Autumn Irisl

Strip sets combine to create a colorful Irish Chain design.

PROJECT NOTE
The fabrics chosen for this project are very close in color, ranging from a light gold to rust, red, brown and green. To avoid confusion, it would be helpful to cut a small swatch of each fabric, label and lay out in numerical order to make a color key.

PROJECT SPECIFICATIONS
Skill Level: Beginner
Quilt Size: 50" x 70"
Block Size: 10" x 10"
Number of Blocks: 15

FABRIC & BATTING
- ⅛ yard light gold print (7)
- ⅓ yard medium gold tonal (6)
- ½ yard rust print (5)
- ½ yard dark green print (1)
- ½ yard orange check (4)
- ¾ yard red print (3)
- ⅞ yard brown dot (2)
- 1⅓ yards green/tan stripe
- 1¾ yards orange plaid
- Backing 56" x 76"
- Batting 56" x 76"

SUPPLIES & TOOLS
- All-purpose thread to match fabrics
- Quilting thread
- Basic sewing tools and supplies

Cutting
1. Cut 2½" by fabric width strips as follows: six strips fabric 1; 11 strips fabric 2; nine strips fabric 3; six strips fabric 4; five strips fabric 5; three strips fabric 6; and one strip fabric 7.

2. Cut one fabric 1 strip into (16) 2½" x 2½" A squares.

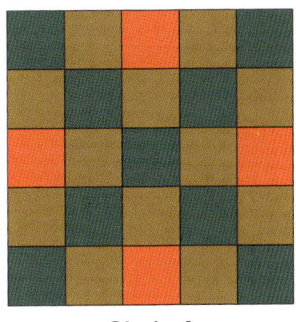

Chain A
10" x 10" Block
Make 8

Chain B
10" x 10" Block
Make 7

3. Cut five 1½" by fabric width strips green/tan stripe. Join strips on short ends to make one long strip; press seams open. Subcut strip into two 58½" B strips and two 40½" C strips.

4. Cut six 5½" by fabric width strips orange plaid. Join strips on short ends to make one long strip; press seams open. Subcut strip into two 60½" D strips and two 50½" E strips.

5. Prepare 255" (2¼"-wide) bias strips from orange plaid for binding.

Completing the Blocks
1. Join the 2½" strips with right sides together along the length to make one each strip sets T–Y and two Z strip sets as shown in Figure 1. For strip sets T, V, W and Y, press seams away from the center strip. For strip sets U, X and Z, press seams toward center strip.

2. Subcut strip sets into 2½" segments, again referring to Figure 1. You will need 16 each T and U, eight V, 14 each W and X, seven Y and 32 Z segments.

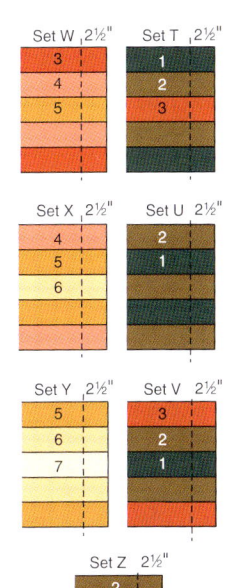

Figure 1

3. Arrange five strip sets to make a Chain A block as shown in Figure 2; join to complete one block. Press seams in one direction. Repeat to make eight Chain A blocks.

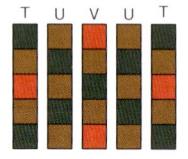

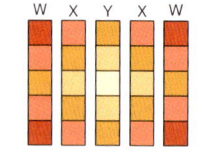

Figure 2

Figure 3

4. Repeat step 3 to make a Chain B block as shown in Figure 3; press seams in the opposite direction from A blocks. Repeat to make seven Chain B blocks.

Completing the Top

1. Join two A blocks with one B block and four Z segments to make an X row as shown in Figure 4; press seams toward Z segments. Repeat to make three X rows.

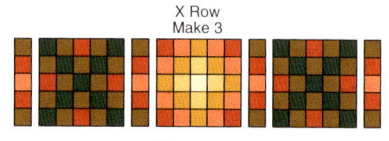

Figure 4
X Row Make 3

2. Join two B blocks with one A block and four Z segments to make a Y row as shown in Figure 5; press seams toward Z segments. Repeat to make two Y rows.

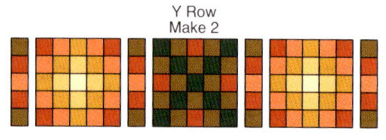

Figure 5
Y Row Make 2

3. Join three Z segments with four A squares to make a sashing row as shown in Figure 6; press seams toward the Z segments. Repeat to make four sashing rows.

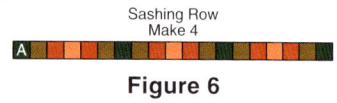

Figure 6
Sashing Row Make 4

4. Arrange and join the X and Y rows with the sashing rows referring to the Placement Diagram for positioning of rows; press seams toward the sashing rows.

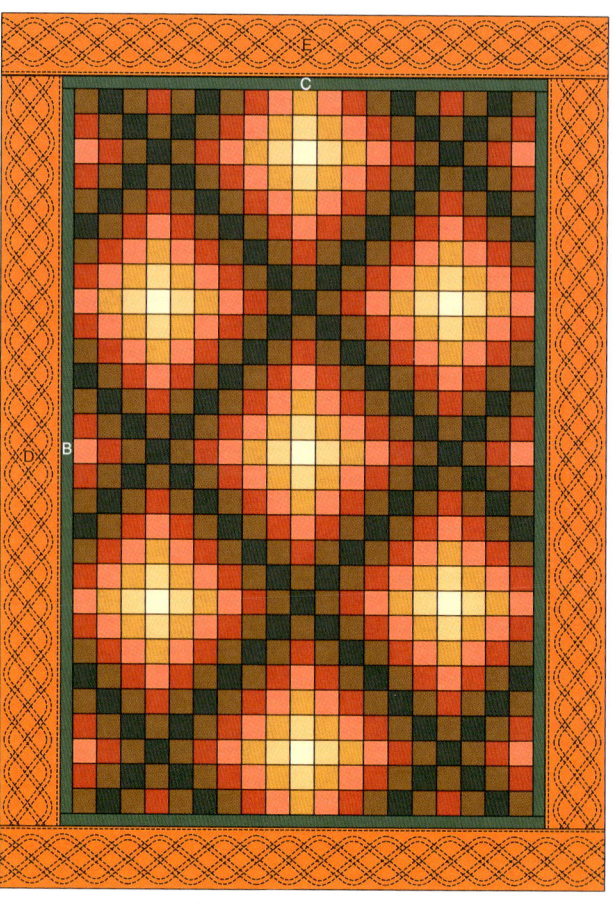

Autumn Irish Chain
Placement Diagram
50" x 70"

Color Key
- Dark green (1)
- Brown (2)
- Red (3)
- Orange check (4)
- Rust (5)
- Medium gold (6)
- Light gold (7)

5. Sew B strips to opposite long sides and C strips to the top and bottom of the pieced center; press seams toward the B and C strips.

6. Sew D strips to opposite long sides and E strips to the top and bottom of the pieced center to complete the top; press seams toward the D and E strips.

Completing the Quilt

1. Mark for quilting. **Note:** *Patterns are given for the block and border quilting designs used on the sample quilt.*

2. Sandwich the batting between the completed top and prepared backing piece; pin or baste to hold.

3. Quilt as desired by hand or machine. When quilting is complete, trim edges even and remove pins or basting.

4. Join binding strips on short ends to make one long strip; press seams open.

5. Fold the binding strips with wrong sides together along the length; press.

6. Pin binding to the quilted top with raw edges even; stitch all around, mitering corners and overlapping ends.

7. Turn the binding to the wrong side; hand- or machine-stitch in place to finish. ■

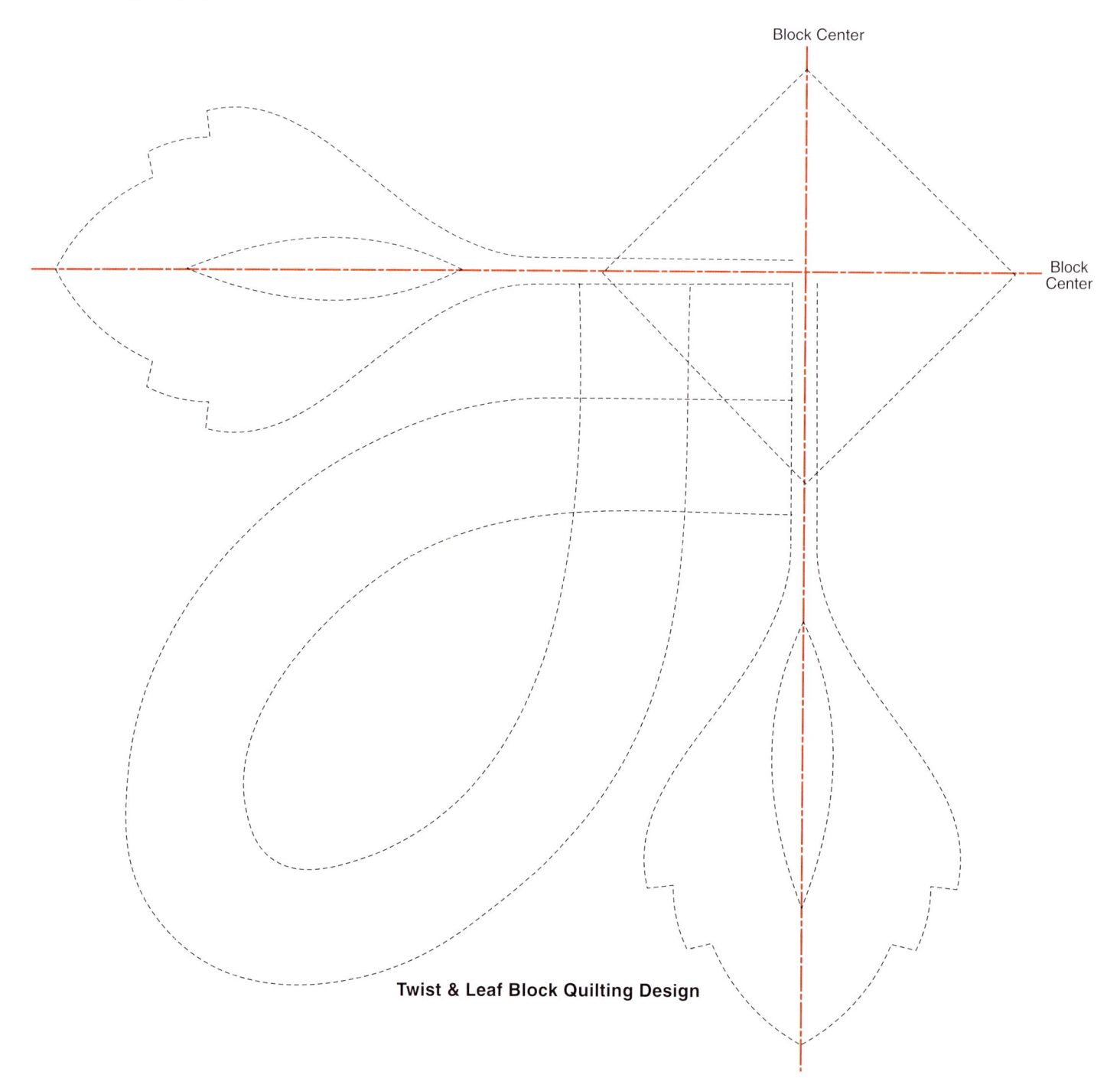

Block Center

Block Center

Twist & Leaf Block Quilting Design

Ends of side borders

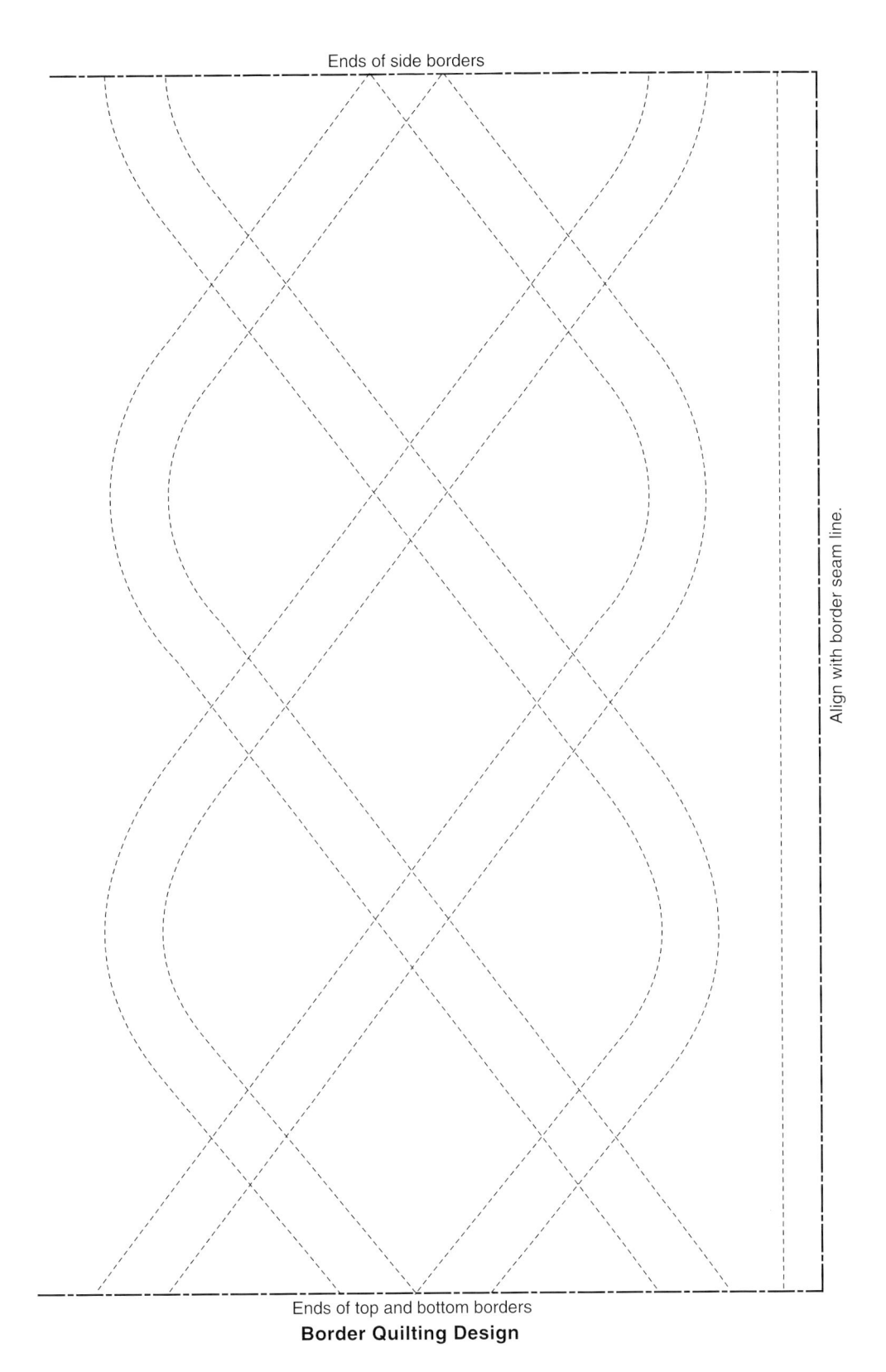

Align with border seam line.

Ends of top and bottom borders

Border Quilting Design

Leaf & Vine Runner

Tiny berries accent these autumn leaves.

PROJECT SPECIFICATIONS
Skill Level: Intermediate
Runner Size: 41¾" x 12"
Block Size: 3" x 3"
Number of Blocks: 8

FABRIC & BATTING
- Scraps dark purple and 4 different rust prints
- Fat quarter brown mottled
- ⅛ yard purple/rust stripe
- ½ yard multicolor autumn print
- ½ yard tan mottled
- Backing & Batting 46" x 16"

SUPPLIES & TOOLS
- All-purpose thread to match fabrics
- Quilting thread
- Paper
- Card stock
- 1 dime
- ¼" bias bar
- Tweezers
- Basic sewing tools and supplies

Cutting
1. Make five copies of the leaf paper-piecing patterns given. Cut one copy of each block apart on solid lines; cut fabric pieces using the paper pieces, adding at least ¼" all around. Fold B horizontally and vertically; crease to mark centers.

2. Cut eight 3½" x 3½" A squares, one 6½" x 6½" B square and one 5⅛" x 5⅛" C square tan mottled. Cut the C square in half on one diagonal to make two C triangles.

3. Cut two 1½" x 32" D strips tan mottled.

4. Cut two 1" x 29" E strips, two 1" x 7" F strips and two 1" x 7½" G strips purple/rust stripe.

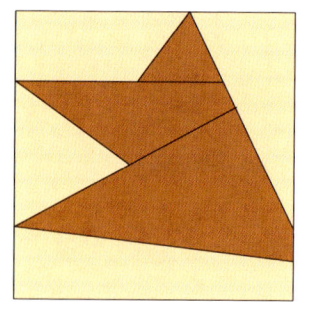

Leaf
3" x 3" Block
Make 4

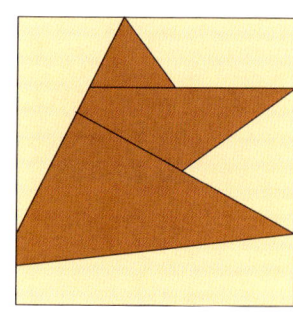

Reverse Leaf
3" x 3" Block
Make 4

5. Cut two each 2" x 32" H, 2" x 9" I and 2" x 10" J strips multicolor autumn print.

6. Cut three 2¼" by fabric width strips multicolor autumn print for binding.

7. Prepare two (18") 1⅛"-wide bias vine strips brown mottled.

8. Cut one 3½" x 3½" K square dark purple print; fold square and crease to mark the vertical and horizontal centers.

9. Trace around the dime on card stock 20 times; cut out on traced line. Repeat on the wrong side of the dark purple print, adding ¼" around the traced line when cutting.

Completing the Blocks
1. Refer to Paper-Piecing Instructions on page 47 and Figures 1 and 2 to complete four Leaf and four Reverse Leaf blocks.

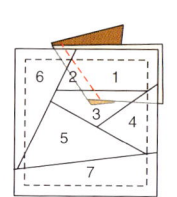

Figure 1

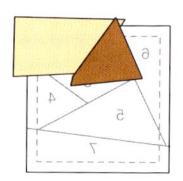

Figure 2

6 Autumn Harvest Quilts HOUSE OF WHITE BIRCHES, BERNE, INDIANA 46711 DRGNETWORK.COM

Completing the Top

1. Sew an A square to a Leaf block to make an A unit as shown in Figure 3; press seam toward A. Repeat for four A units.

Figure 3

Figure 4

Figure 5

2. Repeat step 1 with A and Reverse Leaf blocks to make four reverse A units referring to Figure 4.

3. Join two A and two reverse A units to make a leaf section as shown in Figure 5; press seams in one direction. Repeat to make two leaf sections.

4. Join the two leaf sections with B and add C to each end referring to Figure 6; press seams toward B and C.

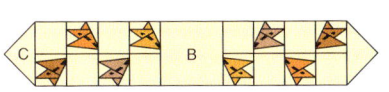

Figure 6

Figure 7

5. Center and sew a D strip to opposite long sides of the pieced center; press seams toward D strips.

6. Trim excess D strips even with the angle of C on each end as shown in Figure 7.

7. Center and sew an E strip to opposite long sides of the pieced center; press seams toward E strips. Trim ends referring to step 6.

8. Add an F strip to each end, matching one end of F to the corner of C; press seams toward F strips and trim as in step 6.

9. Repeat steps 7 and 8 with G, H, I and J strips to complete the pieced top referring to the Placement Diagram for positioning of strips.

Completing the Appliqué

1. Fold each 18" bias vine strip in half along the length with wrong sides together; stitch. Trim seam to 1/8", insert bias bar and press to complete the vine strips.

2. Using the vine appliqué layout guide given, arrange the vine strip on the pieced top and hand-stitch in place.

HOUSE OF WHITE BIRCHES, BERNE, INDIANA 46711 DRGNETWORK.COM

Autumn Harvest Quilts 7

3. Turn under edges of K ¼" all around.

4. Center K diagonally on B using crease marks as guides as shown in Figure 8; hand-stitch in place, being sure to cover the ends of the vine strips.

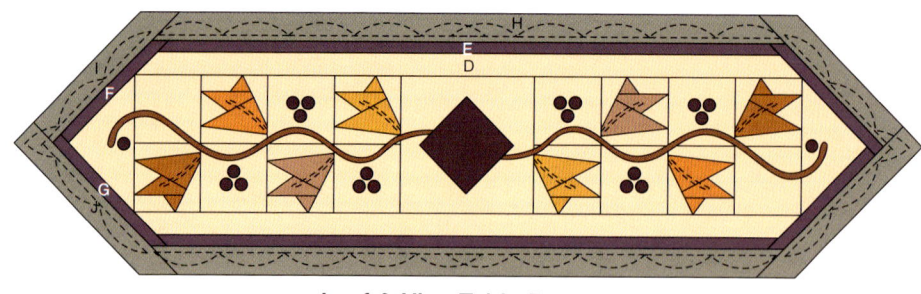

Leaf & Vine Table Runner
Placement Diagram
41¾" x 12"

Figure 8

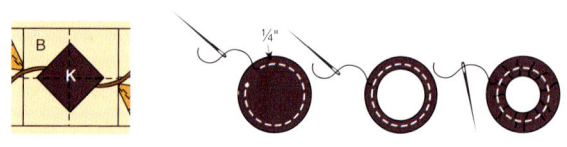

Figure 9

5. To make berries, using a knotted thread, hand-stitch a line of gathering stitches around each berry circle ¼" from edge as shown in Figure 9.

6. Place a card-stock circle inside the stitched line and pull thread to gather fabric around card-stock circle, again referring to Figure 9; secure thread with a backstitch to hold, leaving thread attached.

7. Place the berry on runner top and hand-stitch in place using the same thread end. Repeat to complete and apply 20 berries referring to the Placement Diagram for positioning.

8. Carefully make an X slit in the background fabric within the berry stitching lines on the wrong side of the runner as shown in Figure 10; remove card-stock circles with tweezers.

Figure 10

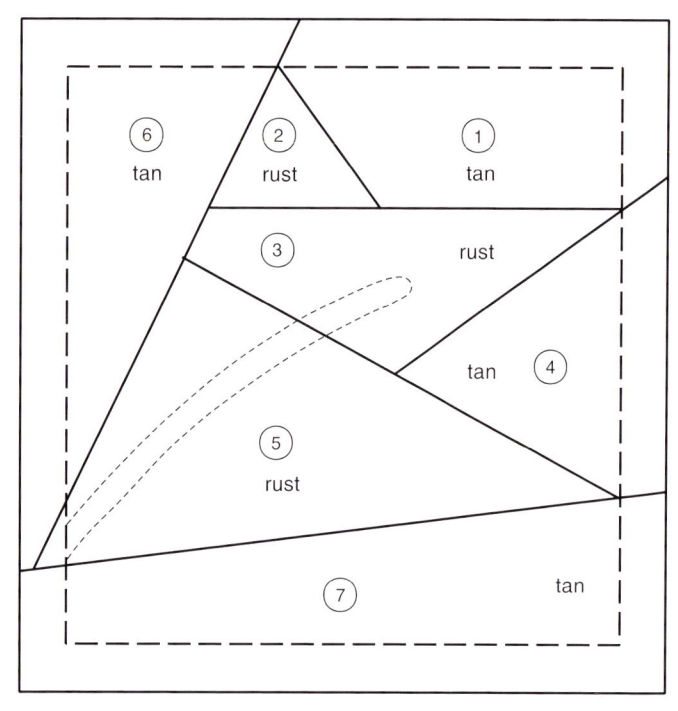

Leaf Paper-Piecing Pattern
Make 5 copies

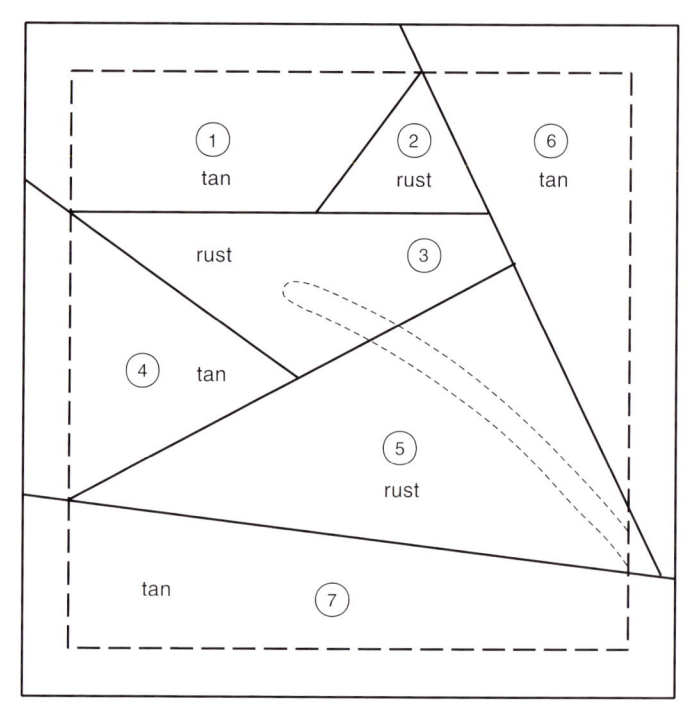

Reverse Leaf Paper-Piecing Pattern
Make 5 copies

Autumn Harvest Quilts HOUSE OF WHITE BIRCHES, BERNE, INDIANA 46711 DRGNETWORK.COM

Completing the Quilt

1. Mark for quilting.

2. Sandwich the batting between the completed top and prepared backing piece; pin or baste to hold.

3. Quilt as desired by hand or machine. When quilting is complete, trim edges even and remove pins or basting.

4. Join binding strips on short ends to make one long strip; press seams open.

5. Fold the binding strips with wrong sides together along the length; press.

6. Pin binding to the quilted top with raw edges even; stitch all around, mitering corners and overlapping ends.

7. Turn the binding to the wrong side; hand- or machine-stitch in place to finish. ■

Vine Appliqué Layout Guide
Middle and end section shown. For center section, repeat the section between the *'s. Align dashed lines with seams of background. Place berry clusters at each outward curve on the A squares.

HOUSE OF WHITE BIRCHES, BERNE, INDIANA 46711   DRGNETWORK.COM   Autumn Harvest Quilts

Oak & Acorn Pillow

One appliqué block makes a perfect accent pillow.

Oak & Acorn
10" x 10" Block

PROJECT SPECIFICATIONS
Skill Level: Intermediate
Pillow Size: 16" x 16"
Block Size: 10" x 10"
Number of Blocks: 1

FABRIC & BATTING
- 2 homespun dishtowels in autumn tartan colors
- 2 (5½" x 5½") H squares each 2 different tan prints
- Scraps brown tonal, brown plaid and medium and dark rust and hunter green prints

SUPPLIES & TOOLS
- All-purpose thread to match fabrics
- Quilting thread
- Hunter green embroidery floss
- 16" square pillow form
- 4 rust/red ¾" buttons
- 1¼ yards 1⅜"-wide tan jumbo rickrack
- 1¼ yards ⅛"-wide poly cording for piping
- Zipper foot
- Basic sewing tools and supplies

Cutting
1. Cut one 16½" x 16½" A square from one homespun dishtowel for pillow front; fold and crease to match the horizontal and vertical centers. **Note:** *When cutting panels from homespun towels, center plaid on front and match plaid repeat for back halves.*

2. Cut one each 9⅞" x 16½" B back panel, 8⅛" x 16½" C back panel, 1¾" x 16½" D facing strip, and 3½" x 16½" E placket and two each 2" x 7¼" F ties and 2" x 5¼" G ties from the second homespun towel and the remainder of the first towel.

3. Prepare templates for appliqué shapes using patterns given. Cut acorn pieces as directed on each piece, adding a ¼" seam allowance all around when cutting.

4. Cut one 2¼" x 22" I strip each brown tonal and brown plaid for oak leaf halves.

5. Prepare a 45" length of ⅞"-wide hunter green bias.

Completing the Block
1. Join the H squares as shown in Figure 1 to make the block background; press seams in rows in opposite directions. Fold and crease to mark the diagonal centers.

Figure 1

2. Join the I strips along the length to make a strip set; press seam toward the brown tonal side.

3. Align the oak leaf template with the seam line between the two strips; cut out four leaf shapes, leaving a ¼" seam allowance all around.

4. Turn under the edges of all appliqué pieces; baste to hold.

5. Arrange one oak leaf on each creased diagonal center line 1" from the center; hand-stitch in place.

10 Autumn Harvest Quilts HOUSE OF WHITE BIRCHES, BERNE, INDIANA 46711 DRGNETWORK.COM

6. Center and stitch the acorn and acorn top on top of the leaf ends to complete the block.

Completing the Pillow Front

1. Wrap the bias around the ⅛"-wide poly cord; stitch close to cording using a zipper foot to make piping as shown in Figure 2.

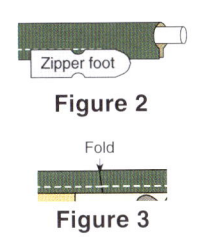

Figure 2

Figure 3

2. Sew the piping around the edges of the appliquéd block, butting cord at the beginning and end; fold under fabric end and overlap as shown in Figure 3.

3. Press under the raw edges of the appliquéd block as shown in Figure 4; baste to hold.

Figure 4

4. Center and pin the piped block to A.

5. Starting at one corner and leaving a 1" excess, arrange and pin the jumbo rickrack under the edge of the piped block around all sides, pleating at corners and exposing approximately half of the rickrack width as shown in Figure 5. **Note:** Take care to balance the repeat on each side. Fold under and overlap the end over the beginning as shown in Figure 6.

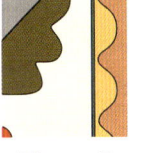

Figure 5

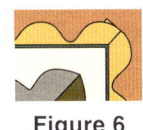

Figure 6

6. Topstitch close to the piped edge of the block through all layers with thread to match fabric.

7. Quilt as desired by hand or machine. **Note:** The pillow shown was hand-quilted with contrasting thread in the ditch of the H squares and around appliqué shapes.

8. Using hunter green embroidery floss, sew a rust/red ¾" button 2" in from edges centered over the H seams to complete the pillow top.

Completing the Pillow

1. Fold each F and G tie strip in half with wrong sides together along the length; stitch across one end and along the length. Clip corners; turn right side out. Press flat with seam on the side to complete the ties.

2. Press under a double 1" hem on the long edge of B. Open flat and position the F ties 5" from the short sides with raw edges ¾" from one long side raw edge as shown in Figure 7; refold the double hem and topstitch next to hem and panel edges, enclosing the tie raw ends as shown in Figure 8.

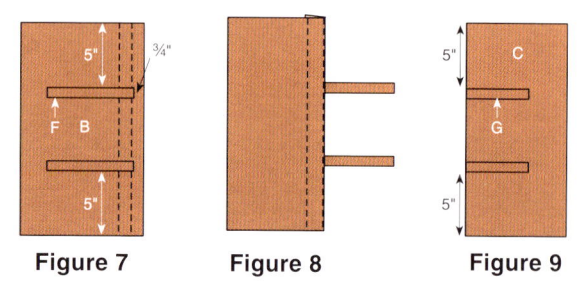

Figure 7   Figure 8   Figure 9

3. Position and pin the G ties 5" from short sides of C with tie raw edges even with long edge of C as shown in Figure 9.

4. Press E in half along length with wrong side together. Align the raw edges of E with the raw edge of C; pin and baste with ties between.

5. Press under ¼" on one long edge of the D facing strip. Pin to the basted E-C unit with raw, unfolded edge of D even with the edge of the basted unit; stitch as shown in Figure 10.

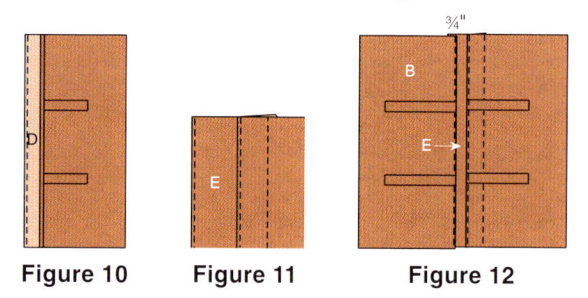

Figure 10   Figure 11   Figure 12

6. Turn and press the D facing strip to the wrong side; topstitch close to stitched edge and along the pressed-under edge of D to complete the C right back panel referring to Figure 11.

7. Lay the B and C panels on a flat surface overlapping B ¾" onto the E center placket as shown in Figure 12; baste along the raw edges to hold.

8. Pin the basted back panels right sides together with the finished pillow front; stitch all around. Turn right side out; press edges flat.

9. Insert pillow form and tie the F and G ties in a knot to finish. ■

Leaf template on page 48

Oak & Acorn Pillow
Placement Diagram
16" x 16"

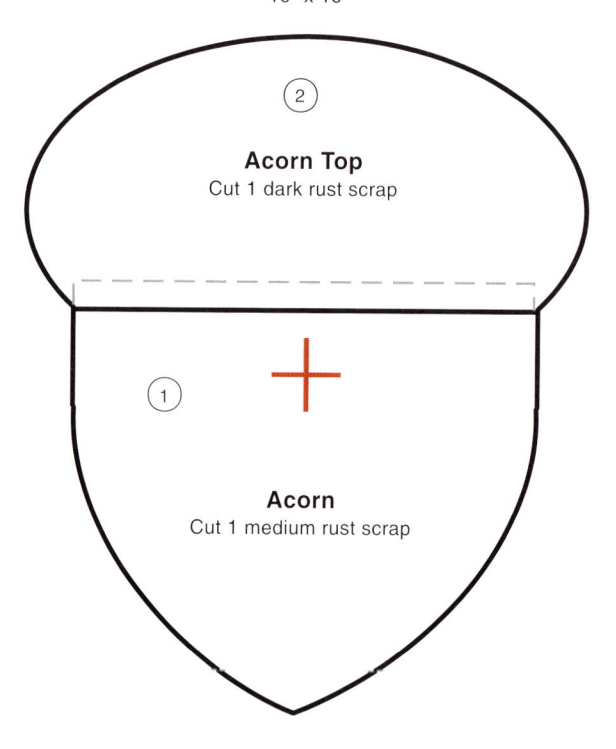

②
Acorn Top
Cut 1 dark rust scrap

①
Acorn
Cut 1 medium rust scrap

12   Autumn Harvest Quilts

Indian Corn Topper

Tiny strip-pieced sections create this harvest table topper.

PROJECT SPECIFICATIONS
Skill Level: Advanced
Topper Size: 23¼" x 23¼"
Block Size: 2" x 2" and 3¾" x 14½"
Number of Blocks: 13 and 4

FABRIC & BATTING
- Scraps cream tonals, stripe and solid
- ⅛ yard rust/gold stripe
- ⅛ yard each light (E) and dark rust (D) prints
- ⅛ yard gold print (F) and black check (B)
- ⅛ yard each dark gray (A) and dark brown solids (C)
- ⅛ yard autumn-color plaid
- ¼ yard brown mottled
- ¾ yard gray/green print
- Backing 28" x 28"
- Batting 28" x 28"

SUPPLIES & TOOLS
- All-purpose thread to match fabrics
- Quilting thread
- Basic sewing tools and supplies

Cutting

1. Cut two 1" x 18½" strips each from fabrics A–F.

2. Cut one 2½" by fabric width strip autumn-color plaid; subcut strip into (12) 2½" H squares.

3. Cut two ⅞" x 10½" I strips and two ⅞" x 11¼" J strips rust/gold stripe.

4. Cut four 4¼" x 8" L strips gray/green print.

5. Cut five ⅞" by fabric width strips brown mottled for corn piecing; subcut strips into eight each 8¼" and 1", 12 each 1½" and 2½", and four each 1¼", 1¾", 2" and 2⅝" strips for corn piecing.

6. Cut one ⅞" by fabric width strip dark brown solid for corn piecing; subcut strip into (44) ⅞" squares for corn piecing.

Calico Kernel
2" x 2" Block
Make 13

7. Cut four 1¾" x 1¾" N squares dark rust print.

8. Cut four 1¼" x 18¾" O, two 1¾" x 21¼" P and two 1¾" x 23¾" Q strips gray/green print.

9. Cut three 2¼" by fabric width strips gray/green print for binding.

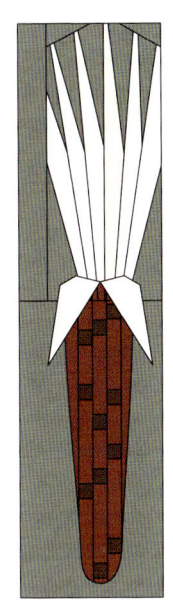

Indian Corn
3¾" x 14½" Block
Make 4

10. Make five copies of the K paper-piecing pattern given. Cut one copy apart on solid lines; use paper pieces to cut fabric pieces, adding at least ¼" all around.

11. Make nine copies of the M paper-piecing pattern given. Cut one copy apart on solid lines; use paper pieces to cut fabric pieces, adding at least ¼" all around.

12. Prepare a template for the leaf using pattern given; cut as directed, adding ⅛"–¼" seam allowance all around when cutting.

Completing the Calico Kernel Blocks

1. Join strips in the following orders to make strip sets as follows: A-B-C-D; E-F-A-B; and C-D-E-F. Press seams in one direction on each strip set.

2. Subcut strip sets into 1" segments as shown in Figure 1.

HOUSE OF WHITE BIRCHES, BERNE, INDIANA 46711   DRGNETWORK.COM

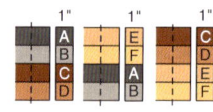

Figure 1

Figure 2

3. Arrange segments to make 13 blocks with four segments in each block referring to Figure 2 for suggestions. **Note:** *Each block will have two of the same segment; turn in opposite directions to vary positioning.*

4. Join the arranged segments to complete 13 Calico Kernel blocks; press seams in one direction.

Completing the Indian Corn Blocks

1. Complete four paper-pieced K sections referring to Paper-Piecing Instructions on page 47 and Figure 3.

Figure 3

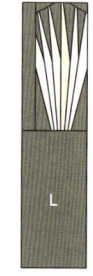

Figure 4

2. Sew a K section to L as shown in Figure 4; press seam toward L. Repeat to make four K/L units.

3. Join the ⅞"-wide pieces to make four of each corn row as shown in Figure 5; trim seams to ⅛" and press seams toward dark brown pieces.

Figure 5

4. Join one of each row as shown in Figure 6; trim seams to ⅛" and press seams in one direction.

5. Sew a ⅞" x 8¼" strip to each long side as shown in Figure 7; trim seams to ⅛" and press seams toward strips.

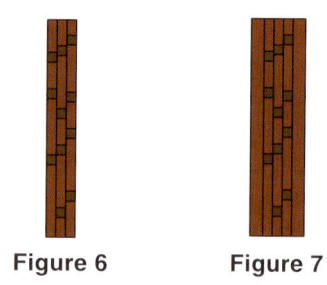

Figure 6

Figure 7

6. Trace a cob shape on the pieced section using the cob appliqué pattern; cut out, leaving a ⅛"–¼" seam allowance all around traced line when cutting. Repeat to cut four cob sections.

7. Turn under the seam allowance all around on each cob section; baste to hold.

8. Referring to the placement line on the K paper-piecing pattern, position and appliqué a cob section to the K/L unit as shown in Figure 8.

9. Turn under seam allowance on leaf pieces and appliqué one leaf and one reverse leaf to the top of the cob on the K/L unit to complete one Indian Corn block; repeat to make four blocks.

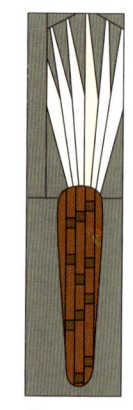

Figure 8

Completing the Top

1. Join three Calico Kernel blocks with two H squares to make an X row as shown in Figure 9; press seams toward H. Repeat to make three X rows.

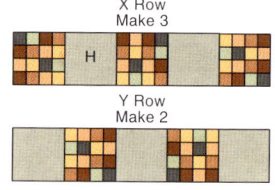

X Row Make 3

Y Row Make 2

Figure 9

2. Join two Calico Kernel blocks with three H squares to make a Y row, again referring to Figure 9; press seams toward H. Repeat to make two Y rows.

3. Join the X and Y rows referring to the Placement Diagram to complete the pieced center; press seams in one direction.

14 Autumn Harvest Quilts   HOUSE OF WHITE BIRCHES, BERNE, INDIANA 46711   DRGNETWORK.COM

4. Sew an I strip to opposite sides and J strips to the remaining sides of the pieced center; press seams toward I and J strips.

5. Match one end of one Indian Corn block with one end of the pieced center as shown in Figure 10.

6. With right sides together, stitch from the matched end to within 2" of the end of the pieced center to make a partial seam referring to Figure 11; press seam toward the block.

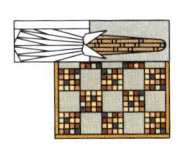

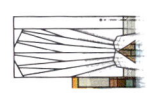

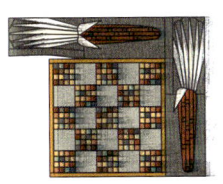

7. Sew a second Indian Corn block to the stitched end of the pieced center as shown in Figure 12; press seam toward the block.

8. Continue to add the remaining blocks around the pieced center; press seams toward block.

9. Complete stitching of the partial seam as shown in Figure 13 and press; remove paper from paper-pieced units.

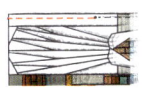

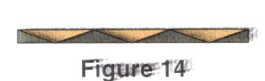

Figure 13   Figure 14

10. Complete eight paper-pieced M sections referring to Paper-Piecing Instructions on page 47 and Figure 14.

Figure 10   Figure 11   Figure 12

11. Join two M sections to make an M strip as shown in Figure 15; press seam in one direction. Repeat to make four M strips.

Figure 15

12. Sew an O strip to the gray/green side of each M strip, again referring to Figure 15; press seams toward O.

13. Sew an M/O strip to opposite sides of the pieced center referring to the Placement Diagram for positioning of strips; press seams toward M/O strips.

14. Sew an N square to each end of each of the remaining M/O strips; press seams away from N. Sew to the top and bottom of the pieced center, again referring to the Placement Diagram for positioning; press seams toward M/N/O strips.

15. Sew P strips to opposite sides and Q strips to the top and bottom of the pieced center to complete the top; press seams toward P and Q strips.

Completing the Topper

1. Sandwich the batting between the completed top and prepared backing piece; pin or baste to hold.

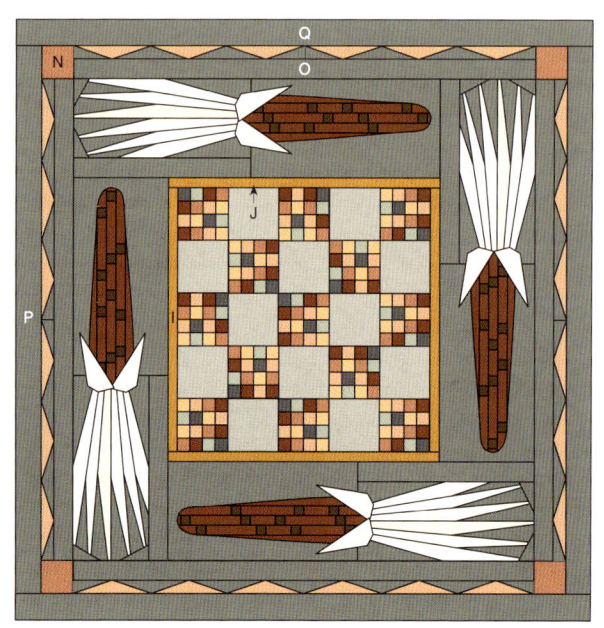

2. Quilt as desired by hand or machine. When quilting is complete, trim edges even and remove pins or basting.

3. Join binding strips on short ends to make one long strip; press seams open.

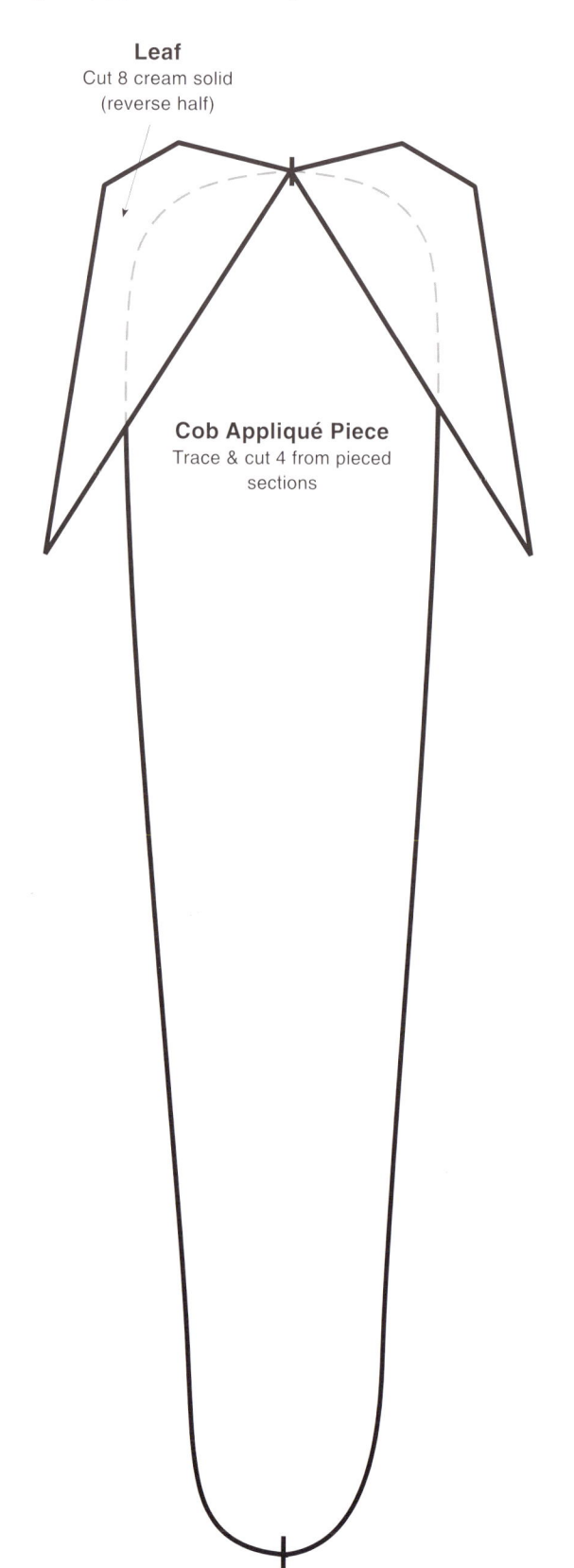

Leaf
Cut 8 cream solid
(reverse half)

Cob Appliqué Piece
Trace & cut 4 from pieced sections

Indian Corn Table Topper
Placement Diagram
23¼" x 23¼"

4. Fold the binding strips with wrong sides together along the length; press.

5. Pin binding to the quilted top with raw edges even; stitch all around, mitering corners and overlapping ends.

6. Turn the binding to the wrong side; hand- or machine-stitch in place to finish.

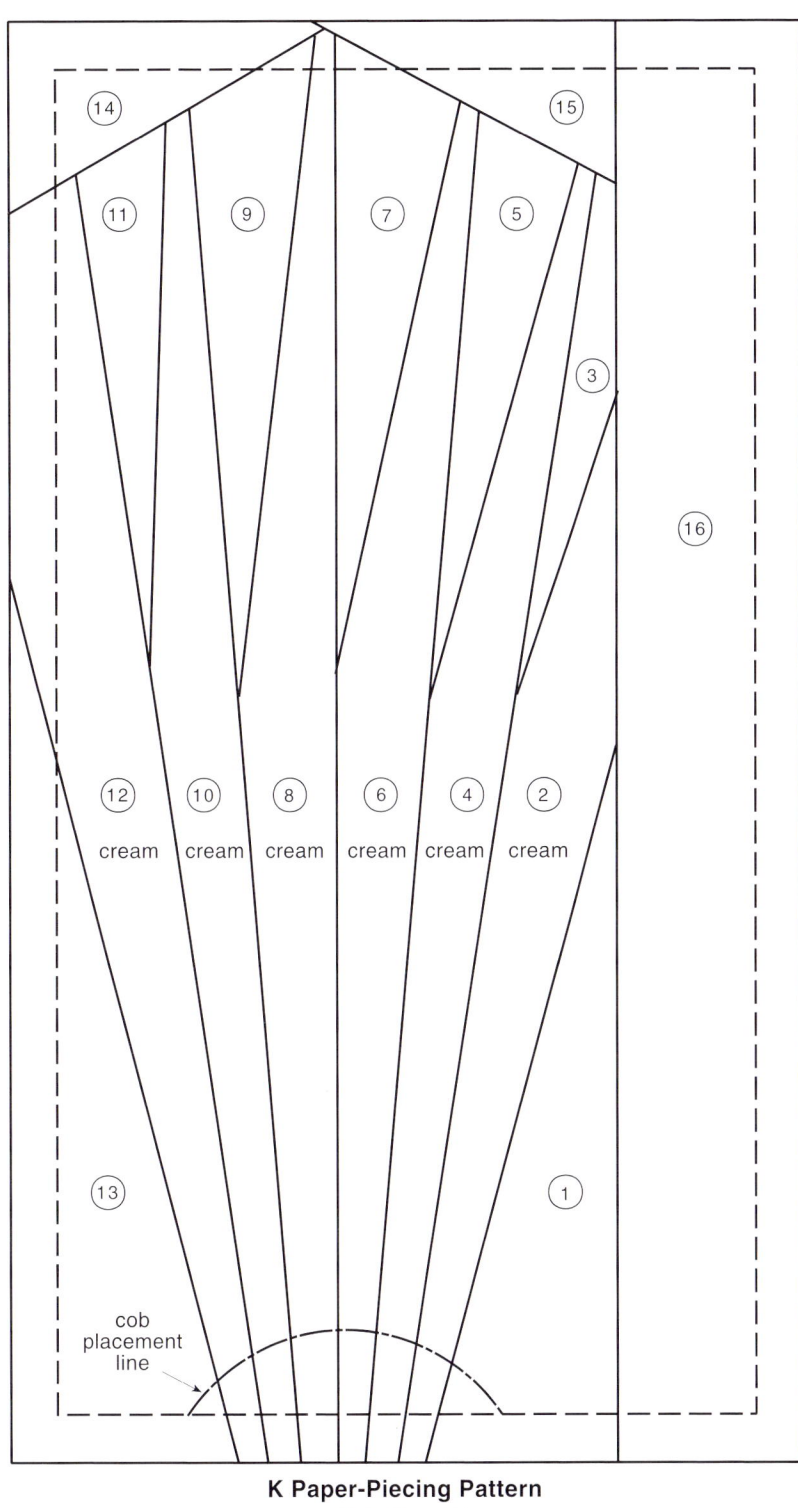

K Paper-Piecing Pattern
Make 5 copies
Use gray/green print for all unlabeled areas.

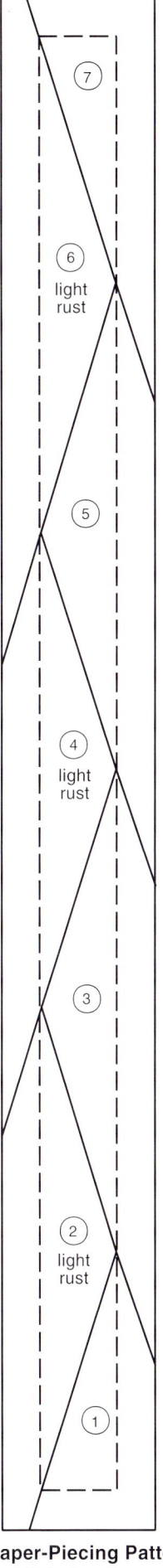

Pieces 2, 4, 6, 8, 10, 12: cream
cob placement line

M Paper-Piecing Pattern
Make 5 copies
Use gray/green print background fabric for all unlabeled areas.

Pieces 2, 4, 6: light rust

Autumn Tie-Ons

Add a quilted seasonal tie-on to jars or pillows.

PROJECT SPECIFICATIONS
Skill Level: Intermediate
Pillow Sleeve Size: 9½" x 8" to fit a 12" x 8" pillow
Jar Sleeve Size: 15" x 7½" (fits 12"-tall x 5½"-diameter jar)

FABRIC & BATTING
- Scraps purple, light, medium and dark green, burgundy and brown
- Scraps 4 different orange prints or tonals
- ⅛ yard white tonal
- ⅛ yard purple metallic
- ¼ yard black tonal
- 1 fat quarter each 2 different orange prints or tonals
- 2 (2" x 16½") L muslin facing strips
- 12½" x 16½" cream prequilted fabric for pillow
- 1 white flannel rectangle each 7" x 8" and 9" x 17"

SUPPLIES & TOOLS
- All-purpose thread to match fabrics
- Contrasting quilting thread
- White embroidery floss
- Polyester fiberfill
- ⅓ yard fusible web
- 1½ yards 1"-wide sheer purple ribbon
- 1½ yards 1½"-wide sheer purple ribbon
- Basic sewing tools and supplies

Cutting

1. Trace appliqué shapes given onto the paper side of the fusible web as directed on patterns for number to cut; cut out shapes, leaving a margin around each one.

2. Bond shapes to the wrong side of fabrics as directed on patterns for color; cut out shapes on traced lines. Remove paper backing.

3. Cut two 5" x 7" A rectangles black tonal.

4. Cut one 1¼" by fabric width strip each black (D) and white (E) tonals. Cut eight 1" x 1⅜" D1 end pieces black tonal.

5. Cut one jar sleeve backing piece 8" x 15½" from one orange fat quarter and a pillow sleeve backing piece 8½" x 10" from the second orange fat quarter.

6. Cut the following strips from purple metallic: four ¾" x 7" B; four ¾" x 5½" C; and two 1½"x 8" J.

7. Cut two of each of the following strips from the orange scraps and remaining orange fat quarters: 1½" x 7½" F; 1¾" x 8½" G; 1¼" x 7½" H; 1¾" x 8" I; and 2¼" x 8" K.

8. Cut four 13" lengths each 1"-wide and 1½"-wide sheer purple ribbon; angle ends.

Completing the A Units

1. Draw a line 1¾" from one long side of A as shown in Figure 1.

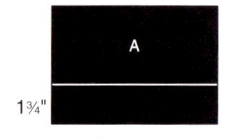

Figure 1

2. Referring to the full-size appliqué motif, arrange appliqué pieces along the drawn line on A in numerical order; when satisfied with placement, fuse in place.

3. Using thread to match fabrics, machine satin-stitch around each shape, again in numerical order. Repeat to make two appliquéd A panels.

4. Transfer the written message to the A piece below the marked line; backstitch along the marked lines using 2 strands white embroidery floss to complete the A panels.

5. Sew B strips to the top and bottom and C strips to opposite long sides of the A panel to complete an A unit; press seams away from A.

6. Sew the D strip to the E strip with right sides together along the length; press seams toward D.

7. Subcut the D-E strip set into (16) 1" D-E units as shown in Figure 2.

Figure 2

8. Join four D-E units on the short ends to make a D-E strip referring to Figure 3; remove the D piece from the end and add a D1 piece to each end to complete the strip, again referring to Figure 3. Repeat to make four D-E strips.

HOUSE OF WHITE BIRCHES, BERNE, INDIANA 46711 DRGNETWORK.COM

Autumn Harvest Quilts 19

Figure 3

Figure 4

9. Sew a D-E strip to opposite long sides of the A unit as shown in Figure 4.

Completing the Pillow

1. Fold the 12½" x 16½" prequilted rectangle in half along the length with right sides together; stitch along three sides, leaving a 4" opening on the long side.

2. Clip corners; turn right side out through the opening and press.

3. Stuff pillow form with polyester fiberfill to desired fullness.

4. Turn the opening seam allowance in ¼"; hand-stitch opening closed.

Completing the Pillow Sleeve

1. Pin the 7" x 8" piece of white flannel to the wrong side of one A unit; quilt around the appliquéd motif and in the ditch of seams. When quilting is complete, trim flannel edges even with the A unit.

2. Sew an F strip to the top and bottom of the A unit to complete the center unit as shown in Figure 5; press seams toward F.

Figure 5

3. Sew a G strip to each short end of the center unit to complete the pieced sleeve top.

4. Sew the 8½" x 10" backing piece to one long side of the sleeve top; press seam toward the backing piece.

5. Center and pin the straight end of each length of 1½"-wide ribbon to each end of the backing and pieced sleeve top; baste to hold in place referring to Figure 6.

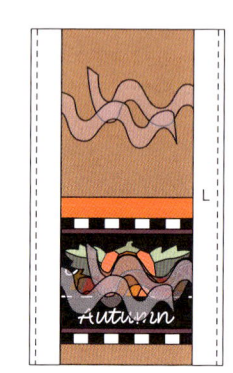

Figure 6

Figure 7

6. Pin and stitch an L facing strip right sides together on each long edge as shown in Figure 7; press seams toward L strips and then to the back side of the stitched unit to finish long edges.

7. Open L strips flat again, align the unstitched short ends of the sleeve top/backing piece and stitch to make a tube as shown in Figure 8; press seam toward the backing piece.

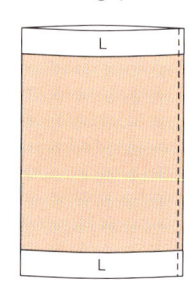

Figure 8

8. Turn right side out; refold the L facing strips to the inside with ribbons extending outside.

9. Slide pillow into the sleeve and center; tie ribbons in a bow at each end to finish.

Completing the Jar Sleeve

1. Sew an H strip to the top and bottom of the remaining A unit; press seams toward H.

2. Sew I, J and K strips to each end of the panel in alphabetical order to complete the jar sleeve top; press seams toward strips as added.

3. Place the completed top right side up on the 9" x 17" rectangle white flannel. Quilt as in step 1 for Completing the Pillow Sleeve; trim white flannel edges even with the top edges.

4. Pin 1"-wide ribbons ⅝" from the edge of each end as shown in Figure 9; baste to hold in place.

Figure 9

5. Place the 8" x 15½" backing piece right side together with the quilted top with ribbon ends inside; trim backing to match the quilted top. Stitch all around, leaving a 4" opening on one side.

6. Clip corners, turn right side out and press flat. Press opening edges to the inside; hand-stitch opening closed to finish. ■

Autumn Tie-On Jar Sleeve
Placement Diagram
15" x 7½"

Autumn Tie-On Pillow Sleeve
Placement Diagram
9½" x 8"

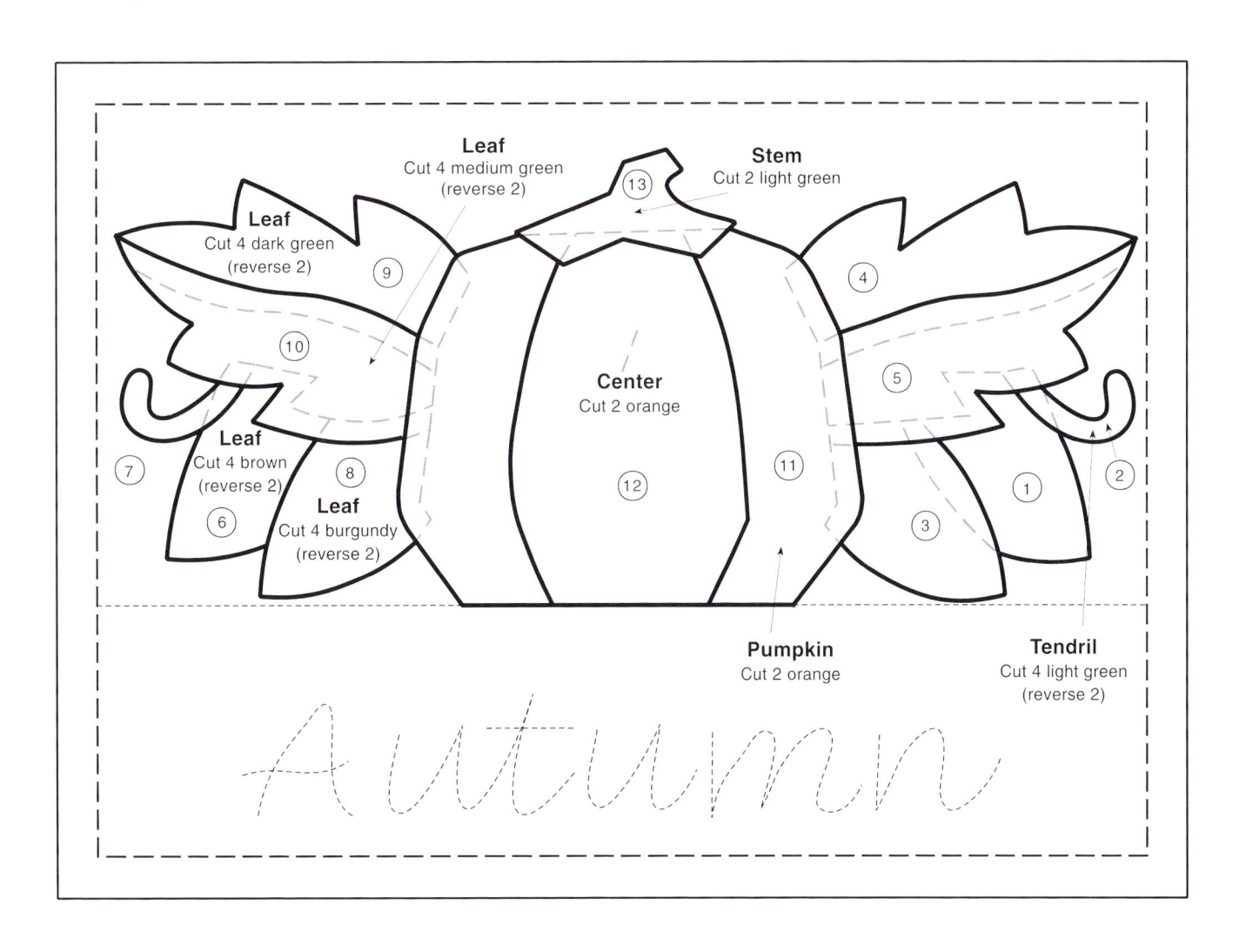

Leaf Cut 4 medium green (reverse 2)

Stem Cut 2 light green

Leaf Cut 4 dark green (reverse 2)

Leaf Cut 4 brown (reverse 2)

Leaf Cut 4 burgundy (reverse 2)

Center Cut 2 orange

Pumpkin Cut 2 orange

Tendril Cut 4 light green (reverse 2)

HOUSE OF WHITE BIRCHES, BERNE, INDIANA 46711 DRGNETWORK.COM

Autumn Harvest Quilts

Autumn Rows Wall Quilt

A variety of pieced motifs combine with appliqué to make this wonderful autumn wall quilt.

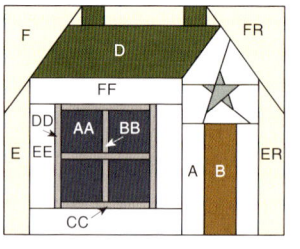

House 11" x 8¾" Block Make 1

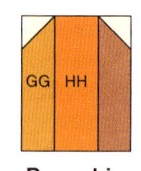

Pumpkin 2½" x 3" Block Make 4

Star 2¼" x 2¼" Block Make 10

PROJECT SPECIFICATIONS
Skill Level: Advanced
Quilt Size: 26" x 40½"
Block Sizes: 11" x 8¾", 2½" x 3", 2¼" x 2¼"
Number of Blocks: 1, 4, 10

FABRIC & BATTING
- Scraps 2 cream and 3 orange prints, brown tonal, dark green check, autumn batik and red solid
- ⅛ yard each dark green print and gray tweed
- ¼ yard dark gray tonal
- ¼ yard medium green tonal
- ¼ yard medium rust print
- ⅔ yard dark olive mottled
- ¾ yard beige mottled
- Backing 32" x 46"
- Batting 32" x 46"

SUPPLIES & TOOLS
- All-purpose thread to match fabrics
- Quilting thread
- Brown and green embroidery floss
- Paper punch
- Card stock
- Basic sewing tools and supplies

Cutting
1. Cut two 1⅜" x 4¾" A rectangles cream print 2.

2. Cut one 1¾" x 4¾" B rectangle brown tonal.

3. Cut four 2⅛" x 2⅛" AA squares, (10) 1¼" x 2¾" P rectangles and (20) 1¼" x 1¼" Q squares dark gray tonal.

4. Cut four ¾" x 2⅛" BB strips, three ¾" x 4" CC strips, two ¾" x 4½" DD strips and four ⅞" x 6" II strips gray tweed.

5. Cut two 1½" x 4½" EE strips and two 1½" x 6½" FF strips cream print 1.

6. Cut the following pieces from beige mottled: one 4¼" x 11½" G; two 5½" x 13" H; four 1½" x 21½" I; one 4" x 5" J; two 3¼" x 4" K; three 1½" x 3½" L; two 3½" x 4½" M; two 3⅜" x 3¾" V; and two 2½" x 21½" W.

7. Cut one 1" by fabric width strip beige mottled; subcut strip into (30) 1" C squares. Draw a diagonal line from corner to corner on the wrong side of each square.

8. Cut two 1" by fabric width strips each beige mottled and gray tweed; subcut strips into (10) 4½" beige and (12) 4½" gray pieces for paper-piecing fence units.

22 Autumn Harvest Quilts HOUSE OF WHITE BIRCHES, BERNE, INDIANA 46711 DRGNETWORK.COM

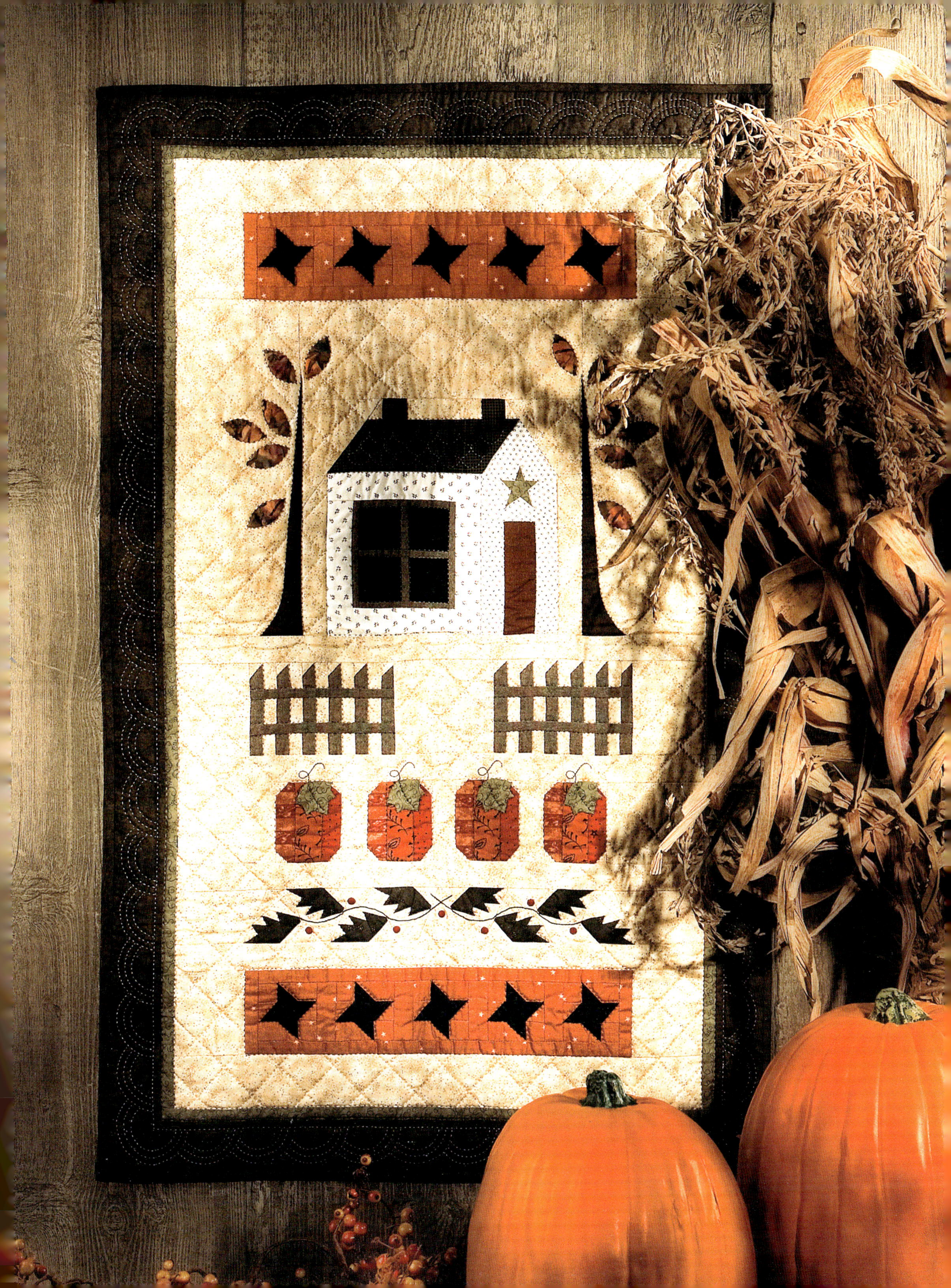

9. Cut the following pieces from medium rust print: (20) 1¼" x 2" R, six 1¼" x 2¾" S, four 1" x 14¾" T and four 1" x 3¾" U.

10. Cut one 1" by fabric width strip medium rust print; subcut strip into (40) 1" RR squares. Draw a diagonal line from corner to corner on the wrong side of 20 RR squares.

11. Cut one 1½" x 16" HH strip from one orange print and one each 1¼" x 16" GG strip from the remaining orange prints.

12. Cut two 1" x 36" X strips and two 1" x 22½" Y strips medium green tonal.

13. Cut two 2½" x 37" Z strips and two 2½" x 26½" ZZ strips dark olive mottled.

14. Cut four 2¼" by fabric width strips dark olive mottled for binding.

15. Prepare templates for pattern pieces given; cut as directed on each piece, adding a ⅛"–¼" seam allowance around appliqué pieces when cutting.

16. Make copies of each of the paper-piecing patterns given as directed. Cut one copy of each house peak, vine and chimney unit apart on solid lines; cut fabric pieces using the cut pieces, adding at least ¼" all around.

Completing the House Strip

1. Sew a BB strip between two AA squares as shown in Figure 1; press seams toward BB. Repeat to make two AA-BB units.

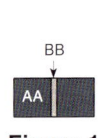

Figure 1

Figure 2

2. Join the two AA-BB units with three CC strips as shown in Figure 2; press seams toward CC.

3. Sew a DD and EE strip to the long sides and FF strips to the remaining sides to complete the window unit as shown in Figure 3; press seams toward DD, EE and FF strips.

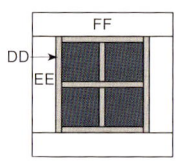

Figure 3

Figure 4

4. Complete paper piecing of each of the three sections of the house peak unit referring to Paper-Piecing Instructions on page 47. Join the sections as shown in Figure 4 to complete the unit.

5. Sew B between two A pieces; press seams toward A.

6. Sew the A-B unit to the house peak unit and add ER as shown in Figure 5; press seam away from A-B and ER.

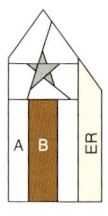

Figure 5

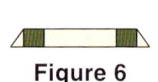

Figure 6

7. Complete paper piecing of the chimney unit referring to Paper-Piecing Instructions on page 47 and referring to Figure 6.

8. To complete the House block, sew E to one EE side of the window unit and add D referring to Figure 7; press seams toward D and E.

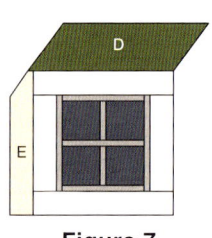

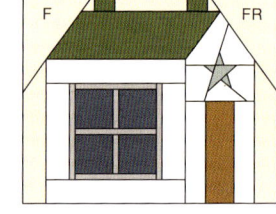

Figure 7

Figure 8

9. Sew the chimney unit to the D side and the house peak unit to the remaining EE side of the window unit as shown in Figure 8; press seams toward D and the house peak unit.

10. Sew F and FR to the corners of the pieced unit to complete the House block, again referring to Figure 8.

11. Remove paper backing from the paper-pieced sections.

12. Turn under the edges of the trunk and leaf pieces and the curved edge only of each tree piece; arrange and hand-appliqué on H and G as shown in Figure 9.

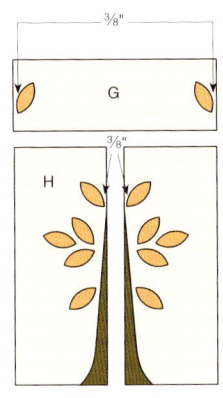

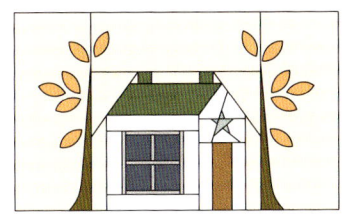

Figure 9

Figure 10

13. Sew G to the top of the House block and H to opposite sides to complete the house strip as shown in Figure 10.

Completing the Fence Strip

1. Complete paper piecing of two fence units using the previously cut 1"-wide strips gray tweed and beige mottled and 12 of the marked C squares referring to Paper-Piecing Instructions on page 47 and Figure 11.

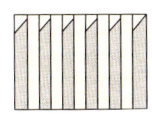

Figure 11

Figure 12

2. Trim the completed units on the outer solid line.

3. Cut each unit along length 1¼" from bottom edge and 1½" from top edge as shown in Figure 12; remove paper.

4. Join the cut sections from one fence unit with two II strips to complete a fence unit as shown in Figure 13; press seams toward II. Repeat to complete two fence units.

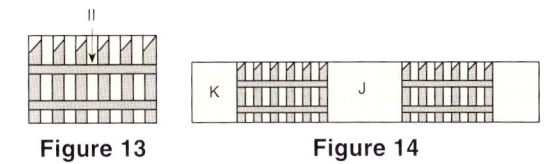

Figure 13

Figure 14

5. Join the fence units with J and add K to each end to complete the fence strip as shown in Figure 14; press seams toward J and K.

Completing the Pumpkin Strip

1. To complete one Pumpkin block, sew HH between two GG strips as shown in Figure 15; press seams toward HH. Cut the pieced strip into four 3½" units, again referring to Figure 15.

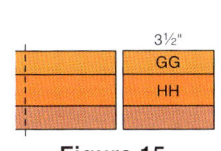

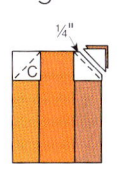

Figure 15

Figure 16

2. Place a C square right sides together on two adjacent corners of a GG-HH unit and stitch on the marked lines as shown in Figure 16.

3. Trim seam allowance to ¼" and press C to the right side to complete one Pumpkin block as shown in Figure 17. Repeat to make four Pumpkin blocks.

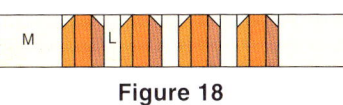

Figure 17

Figure 18

4. Join the blocks with three L strips and add M to the ends to complete the pumpkin strip as shown in Figure 18; press seams toward L and M.

Completing the Vine Strip

1. Complete paper-piecing of four vine and four reversed vine units referring to Paper-Piecing Instructions on page 47.

2. Join four units to make a strip as shown in

Figure 19; press seams in one direction. Repeat to make a reversed strip.

Figure 19

3. Join the two strips with N and add O and OR to the ends to complete the vine strip as shown in Figure 20; press seams toward N, O and OR.

Figure 20

4. To make berries, cut out seven circles from card stock using paper punch.

5. Cut seven fabric circles from red solid using one card-stock piece for pattern, adding ⅛"–¼" all around when cutting fabric.

6. To prepare circle appliqué, baste around edges from the right side using a piece of knotted matching thread.

7. Referring to Figure 21, place a card-stock circle inside a basted fabric circle and pull the thread to gather fabric around card-stock circle; backstitch to secure, leaving thread attached.

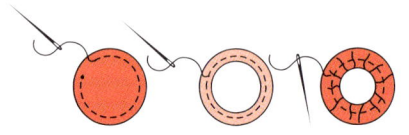

Figure 21

8. Transfer vine and berry placement lines to the completed strip using the vine embroidery guide pattern.

9. Place the berry on each paper-pieced leaf unit referring to close-up photo for positioning; hand-stitch in place. Repeat to make and apply seven berries.

10. Backstitch along marked lines using 2 strands brown embroidery floss to complete the vine strip.

Completing the Star Strip

1. Mark a diagonal line from corner to corner on the wrong side of each Q square.

2. To complete one Star block, place Q right sides together on one end of R and stitch on the marked line referring to Figure 22; trim seam to ¼" and press Q to the right side to complete a Q-R unit. Repeat to make two Q-R units.

Figure 22   **Figure 23**

3. Repeat step 2 with a marked RR square on each end of P to make a P-RR unit referring to Figure 23.

4. Sew RR to the Q end of the Q-R units; press seams toward RR.

5. Join the pieced units as shown in Figure 24 to complete one Star block; press seams toward the P-RR unit. Repeat to make 10 Star blocks.

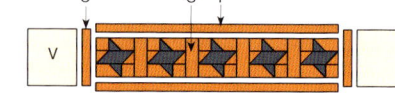

Figure 24   **Figure 25**

6. Join five Star blocks with four S pieces and add T, U and V to complete a star strip as shown in Figure 25; press seams toward S, T, U and V. Repeat to make two star strips.

Completing the Top

1. Arrange the pieced strips with I and W strips as shown in Figure 26; join and press seams toward I and W strips to complete the pieced center.

2. Sew X strips to opposite long sides and Y strips to the top and bottom of the pieced center; press seams toward X and Y strips.

3. Sew Z strips to opposite long sides and ZZ strips to the top and bottom of the pieced center; press seams toward Z and ZZ strips.

Figure 26

5. Fold the binding strips with wrong sides together along the length; press.

6. Pin binding to the quilted top with raw edges even; stitch all around, mitering corners and overlapping ends.

7. Turn the binding to the wrong side; hand- or machine-stitch in place to finish.

4. Prepare and appliqué one pumpkin leaf on the top of each pumpkin block.

5. Transfer stem and vein lines to each leaf using pattern given; backstitch along the stem lines using 2 strands green embroidery floss.

Completing the Quilt

1. Mark the top for quilting. **Note:** *The sample quilt was hand-quilted in the ditch of most seams and using the pattern given on the outside borders.*

2. Sandwich the batting between the completed top and prepared backing piece; pin or baste to hold.

3. Quilt as desired by hand or machine. When quilting is complete, trim edges even and remove pins or basting.

4. Join binding strips on short ends to make one long strip; press seams open.

Autumn Rows Wall Quilt
Placement Diagram
26" x 40½"

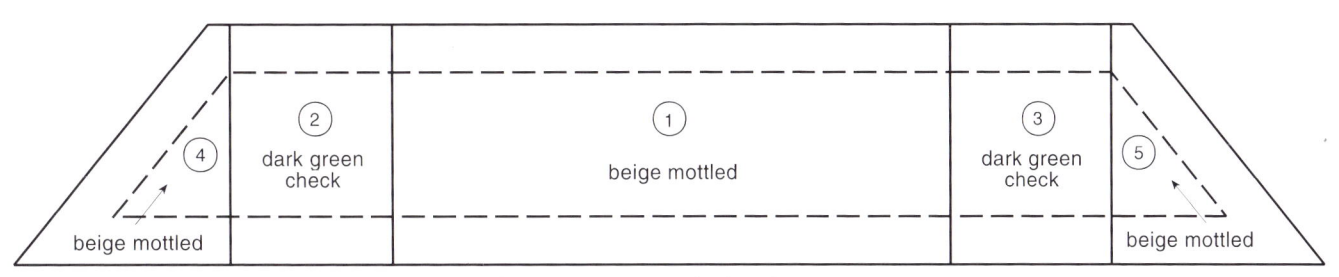

Chimney Paper-Piecing Pattern
Make 2 copies

HOUSE OF WHITE BIRCHES, BERNE, INDIANA 46711 DRGNETWORK.COM   Autumn Harvest Quilts **27**

Center
Berry
Leaf

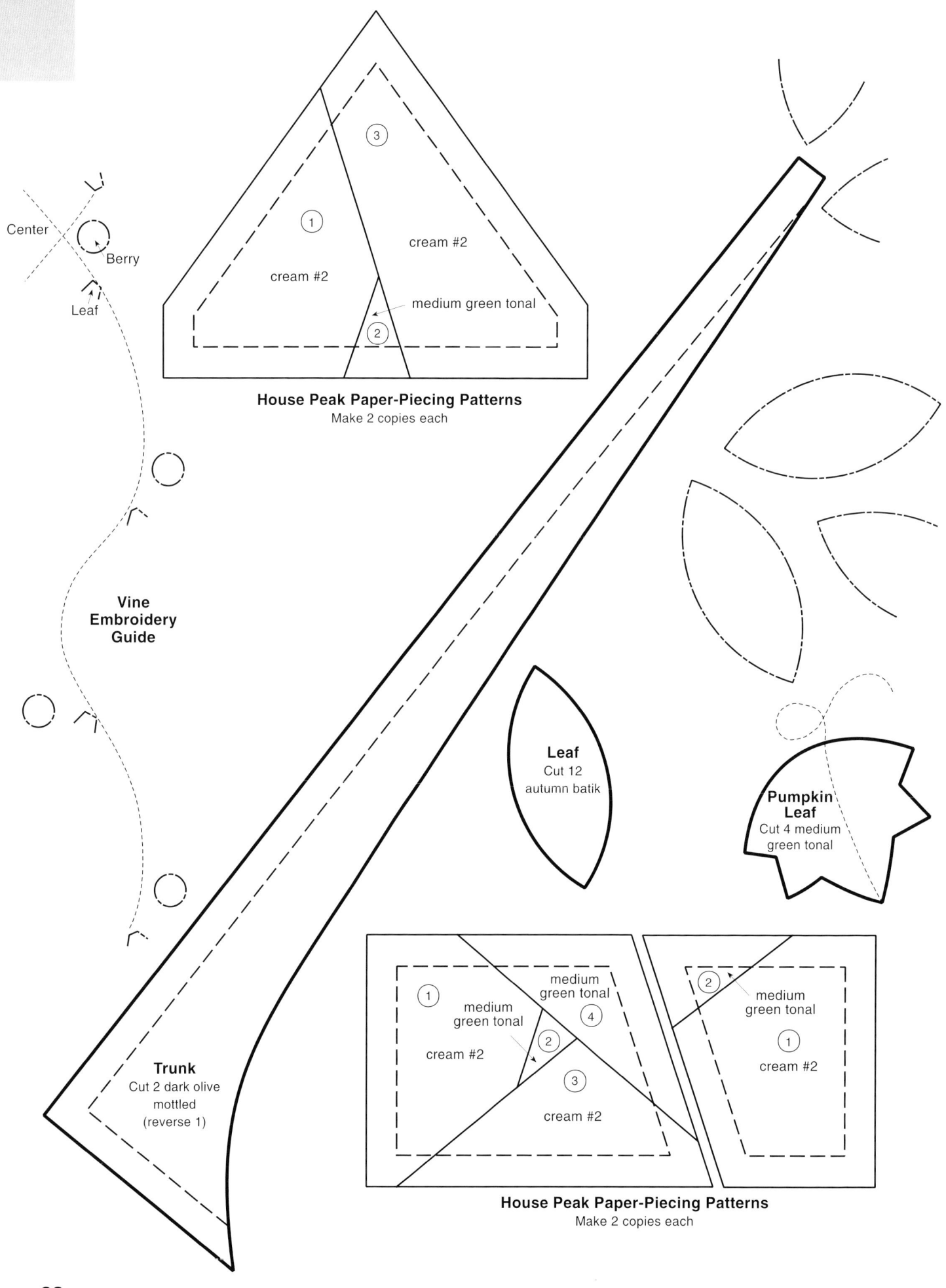

House Peak Paper-Piecing Patterns
Make 2 copies each

cream #2
cream #2
medium green tonal

Vine Embroidery Guide

Leaf
Cut 12 autumn batik

Pumpkin Leaf
Cut 4 medium green tonal

Trunk
Cut 2 dark olive mottled (reverse 1)

House Peak Paper-Piecing Patterns
Make 2 copies each

medium green tonal
medium green tonal
cream #2
cream #2
medium green tonal

28 Autumn Harvest Quilts HOUSE OF WHITE BIRCHES, BERNE, INDIANA 46711 DRGNETWORK.COM

Reversed Vine Paper-Piecing Pattern
Make 5 copies
Use beige mottled for pieces 1, 3, 5 & 8–10
& dark green print for pieces 2, 4, 6 & 7.

Vine Paper-Piecing Pattern
Make 5 copies
Use beige mottled for pieces 1, 3, 5 & 8–10
& dark green print for pieces 2, 4, 6 & 7.

Fence Paper-Piecing Pattern
Make 2 copies

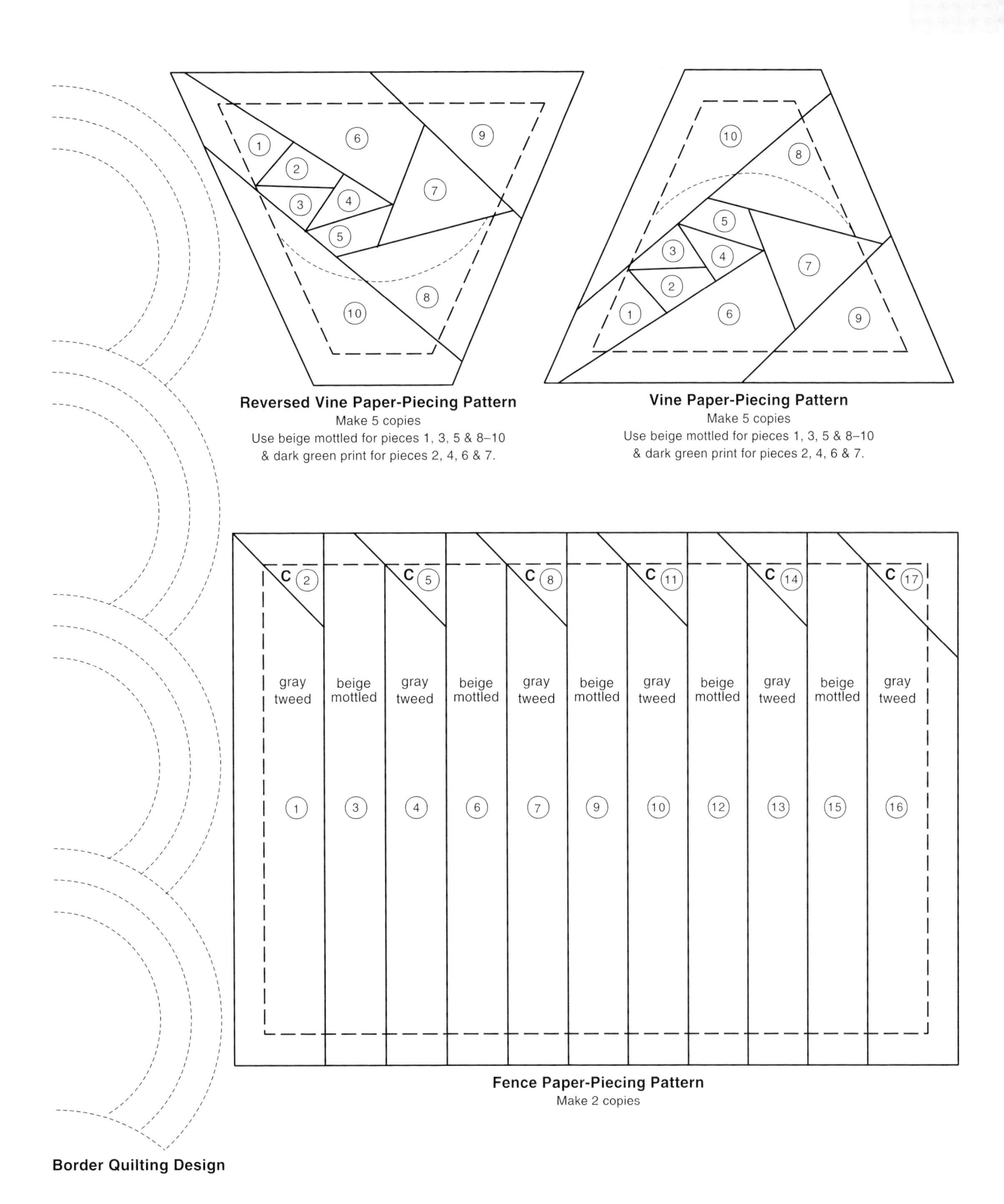

Border Quilting Design

HOUSE OF WHITE BIRCHES, BERNE, INDIANA 46711 · DRGNETWORK.COM

Autumn Harvest Quilts 29

F
Cut 2 beige mottled
(reverse 1)

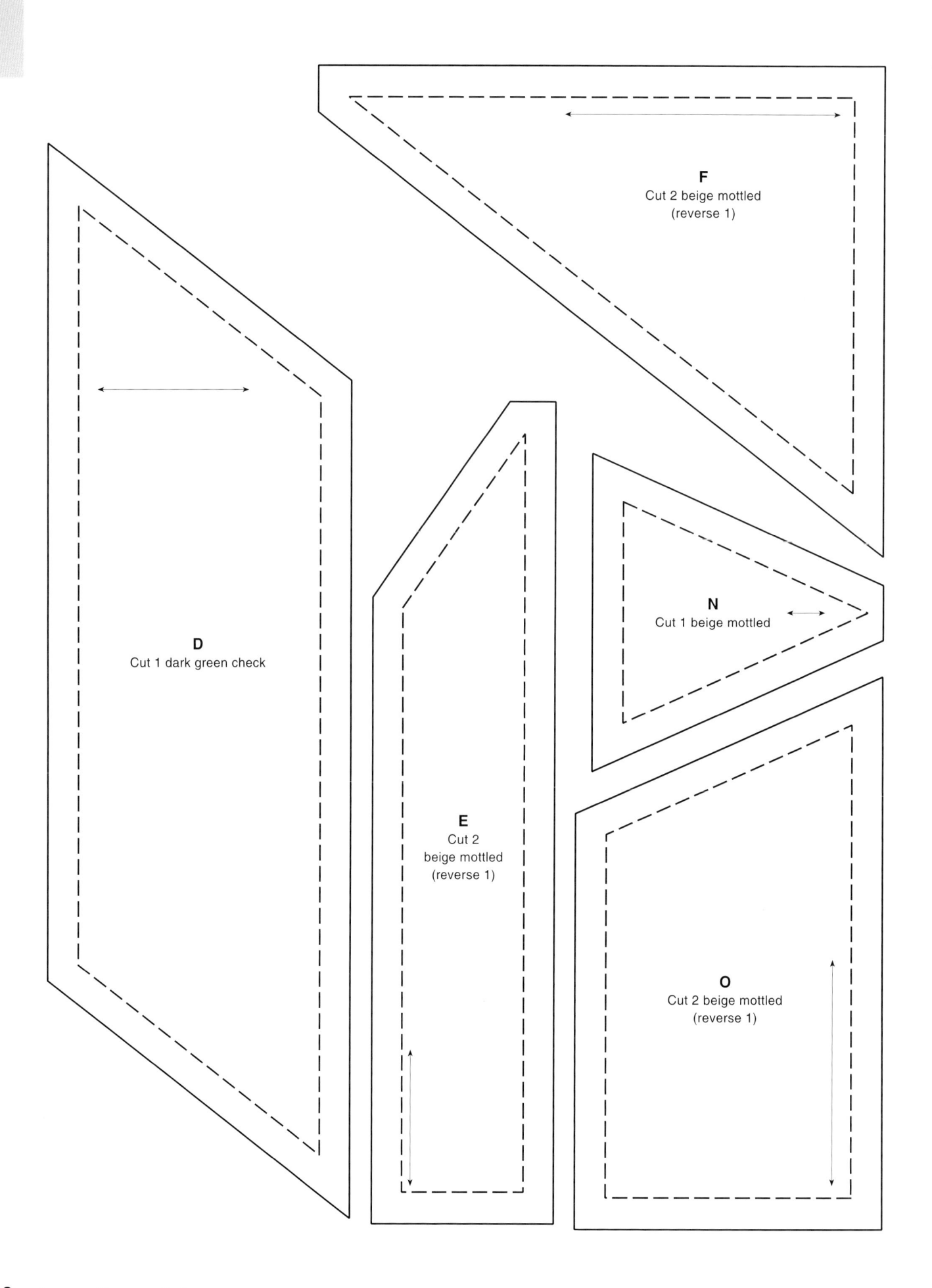

D
Cut 1 dark green check

N
Cut 1 beige mottled

E
Cut 2 beige mottled
(reverse 1)

O
Cut 2 beige mottled
(reverse 1)

Scrappy Leaf Quilt

Scraps in autumn colors float on cream print backgrounds.

PROJECT SPECIFICATIONS
Skill Level: Intermediate
Quilt Size: 75¼" x 86"
Block Size: 7¾" x 7¾"
Number of Blocks: 30

FABRIC & BATTING
- ¼ yard each rust prints 1–3
- ¼ yard each 5 dark purple prints
- ¼ yard each rust prints 4–6
- ½ yard each 6 cream prints
- ⅝ yard olive green mottled
- ¾ yard dark purple pumpkin print
- 1⅛ yards dark green print
- 1⅝ yards medium olive green stripe
- 1⅝ yards medium green tonal
- Backing 81" x 92"
- Batting 81" x 92"

SUPPLIES & TOOLS
- All-purpose thread to match fabrics
- Quilting thread
- Basic sewing tools and supplies

Cutting

1. Prepare templates for H and the stem piece using patterns given; cut as directed on patterns.

2. Cut two 1¾" by fabric width strips each rust prints 1–3; subcut strips into (20) 3" A pieces each fabric.

3. Cut four 1¾" by fabric width strips each rust prints 4 and 5; subcut strips into two 25¼" N strips, two 21⅛" O strips and (20) 3" A pieces each fabric.

4. Cut four 1¾" by fabric width strips rust print 6; subcut strips into four 18½" M strips and (20) 3" A pieces.

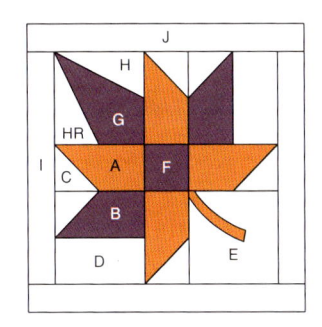

Scrappy Leaf
7¾" x 7¾" Block

5. Cut one 1¾" by fabric width strip each dark purple print and dark purple pumpkin print; subcut strips into (10) 3" B pieces and five 1¾" F squares each fabric.

6. Cut five 3" x 3" G squares each dark purple prints and dark purple pumpkin print.

7. Cut seven 2½" by fabric width strips dark purple pumpkin print. Join strips with right sides together on short ends; press seams open. Subcut strip into two 70½" P and two 63¾" Q strips.

8. Cut three 1¾" by fabric width strips each cream print; subcut strips into (10) 3" D pieces and (30) 1¾" C squares each fabric.

9. Cut four 1¼" by fabric width strips each cream print; subcut strips into (10) 6¾" I strips and (10) 8¼" J strips each fabric.

10. Cut five 3" x 3" E squares each cream print.

11. Cut 22 dark green print (L) and 35 medium green tonal (K) 1½" by fabric width strips.

12. Cut eight 2¼" by fabric width strips olive green mottled for binding.

13. Cut eight 6½" by fabric width strips medium olive green stripe. Join strips with right sides together on short ends; press seams open. Subcut strip into two 74½" R and two 75¾" S strips.

Completing the Blocks

1. Select pieces from one each rust, dark purple and cream prints and group to keep separate; repeat to make six groups.

2. Mark a diagonal line from corner to corner on the wrong side of each C square in one group.

3. Select four A pieces from the same group and referring to Figure 1, place a C square right sides together on one end of A; stitch on the marked line. Trim seam to ¼"; press C to the right side to complete an A-C unit.

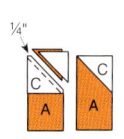

Figure 1

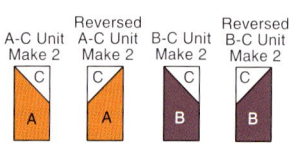

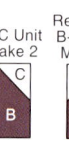

Figure 2

4. Repeat step 3 to make two each A-C and reversed A-C units and B-C and reversed B-C units as shown in Figure 2.

5. Sew an A-C and reversed A-C unit to opposite sides of F to complete the center row as shown in Figure 3; press seams away from F.

Figure 3

6. Turn under edges of one stem piece ¼" along the sides and straight end; baste to hold.

7. Arrange and stitch the stem piece to E referring to the block drawing for positioning.

8. Sew D to a B-C unit as shown in Figure 4; press seam toward D.

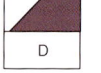

Figure 4

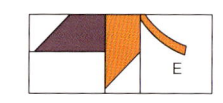

Figure 5

9. Join the appliquéd E square and the B-C-D unit with a reversed A-C unit to complete the bottom row as shown in Figure 5; press seams toward the reversed A-C unit.

10. Referring to the Paper Piecing sidebar on page 35, complete five G-H units of each group as shown in Figure 6; press seams toward H and HR.

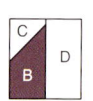

Figure 6

Figure 7

11. Sew a reversed B-C unit to D referring to Figure 7; press seam toward D.

12. Join the G-H unit and the reversed B-C-D unit with an A-C unit to complete the top row as shown in Figure 8, press seams toward the A-C unit.

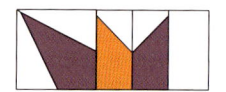

Figure 8

13. Join the rows referring to Figure 9; press seams toward the center row.

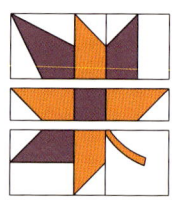

Figure 9

14. Sew I to opposite sides and J to the top and bottom of the pieced center to complete one Scrappy Leaf block; press seams toward I and J. Repeat to make 30 blocks, five from each fabric grouping. Remove paper patterns.

Completing the Quilt

1. Sew an L strip between two K strips with right sides together along the length to make a K-L-K strip set; press seams toward L. Repeat to make 16 strip sets.

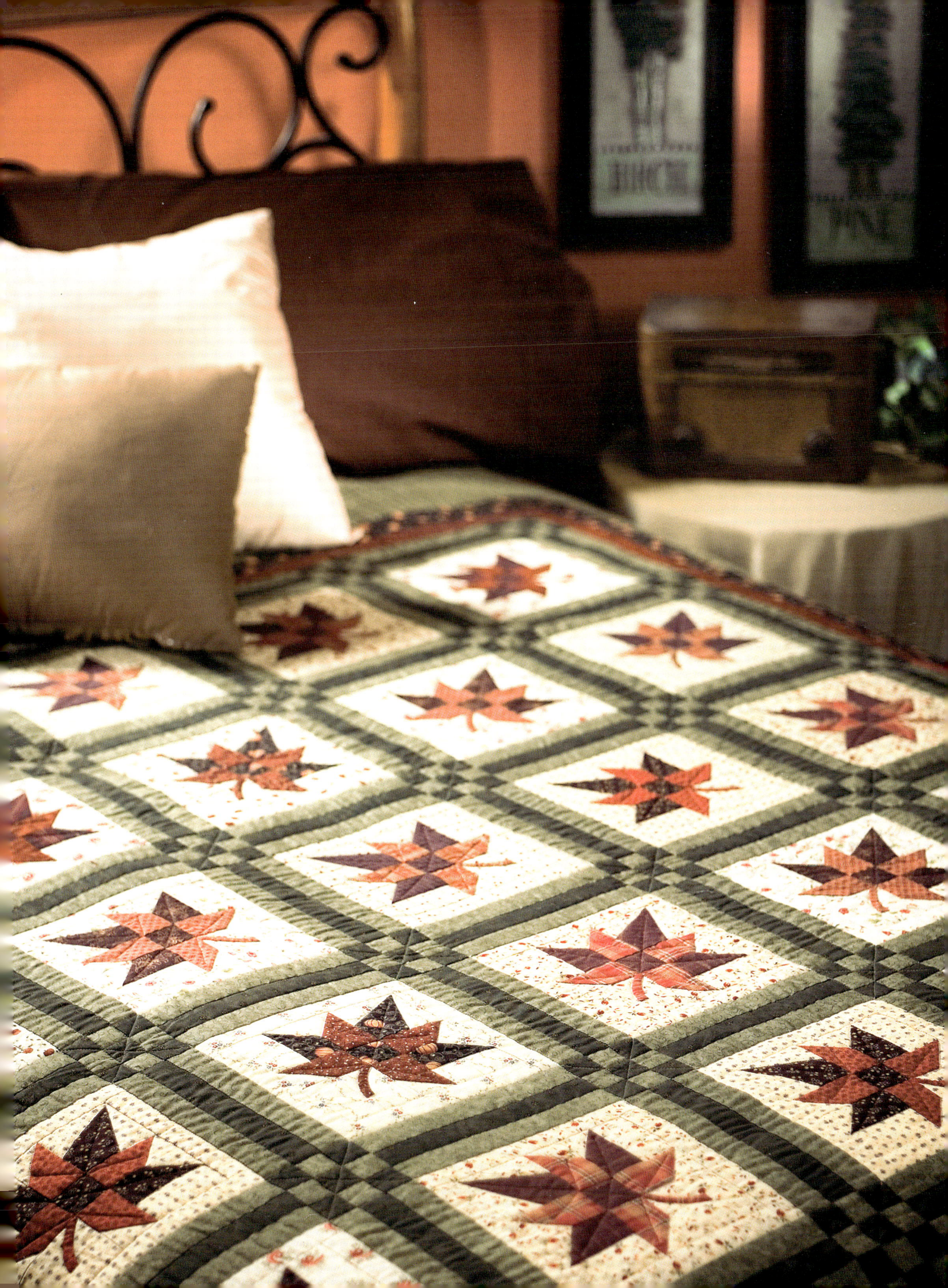

2. Subcut the K-L-K strip sets into (71) 8¼" sashing units and (42) 1½" units as shown in Figure 10.

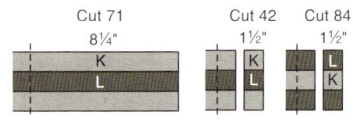

Figure 10

3. Sew a K strip between two L strips with right sides together along the length; press seams toward the L strips. Repeat to make three L-K-L strip sets.

4. Subcut the L-K-L strip sets into (84) 1½" units, again referring to Figure 10.

5. Sew a 1½" L-K-L unit between two 1½" K-L-K units to make a sashing block as shown in Figure 11; press seams toward the K-L-K unit. Repeat to make 42 sashing blocks.

Figure 11

6. Join five Scrappy Leaf blocks with six K-L units to make a row as shown in Figure 12; press seams toward the K-L units. Repeat to make three left-facing rows.

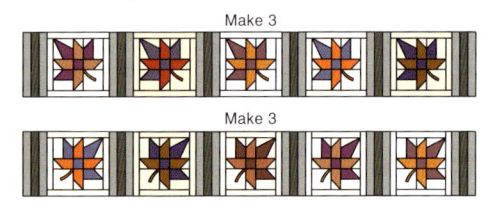

Figure 12

7. Repeat step 6 with five Scrappy Leaf blocks to make three right-facing rows, again referring to Figure 12.

8. Join six sashing blocks with five sashing units to make a sashing row as shown in Figure 13; press seams toward the sashing units. Repeat to make seven sashing rows.

Figure 13

Scrappy Leaf Quilt
Placement Diagram
75¼" x 86"

9. Join the block rows with the sashing rows referring to the Placement Diagram for positioning; press seams toward the sashing rows to complete the pieced center.

10. Sew an M strip between one each rust 4 and rust 5 N strips to make a side strip as shown in Figure 14; press seams toward the N strips. Repeat to make two side strips.

11. Sew an M strip between one each rust 4 and rust 5 O strips to make an end strip, again referring to Figure 14; press seams toward the O strips. Repeat to make two end strips.

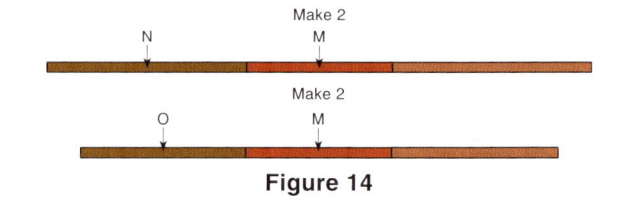

Figure 14

12. Sew the side strips to opposite long sides and the end strips to the top and bottom of the pieced center; press seams toward side and end strips.

34 Autumn Harvest Quilts   HOUSE OF WHITE BIRCHES, BERNE, INDIANA 46711   DRGNETWORK.COM

13. Sew the P strips to opposite long sides and Q strips to the top and bottom of the pieced center; press seams toward the P and Q strips.

14. Sew the R strips to opposite long sides and S strips to the top and bottom of the pieced center; press seams toward the R and S strips.

15. Sandwich the batting between the completed top and prepared backing piece; pin or baste to hold.

16. Quilt as desired by hand or machine. When quilting is complete, trim edges even and remove pins or basting.

17. Join binding strips on short ends to make one long strip; press seams open.

18. Fold the binding strips with wrong sides together along the length; press.

19. Pin binding to the quilted top with raw edges even; stitch all around, mitering corners and overlapping ends.

20. Turn the binding to the wrong side; hand- or machine-stitch in place to finish.

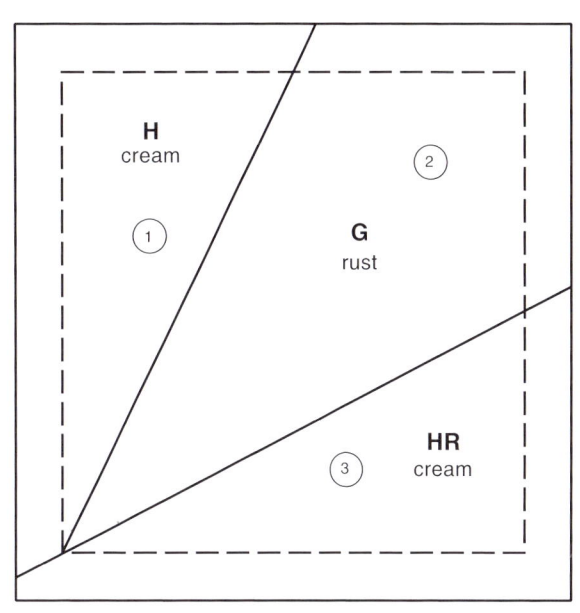

Paper Piecing

1. Make 30 copies of the paper-piecing pattern given.

2. Pin the G square to the unmarked side of a paper-piecing pattern; pin H to G along the line. Turn paper over; stitch on the line between H and G.

3. Turn the paper over; press H to the right side; trim seam allowance to ¼".

4. Repeat with HR on the opposite edge of G.

5. Trim outside edges even with edge of pattern to complete a G-H unit.

G-H Paper-Piecing Unit
Make 30 copies

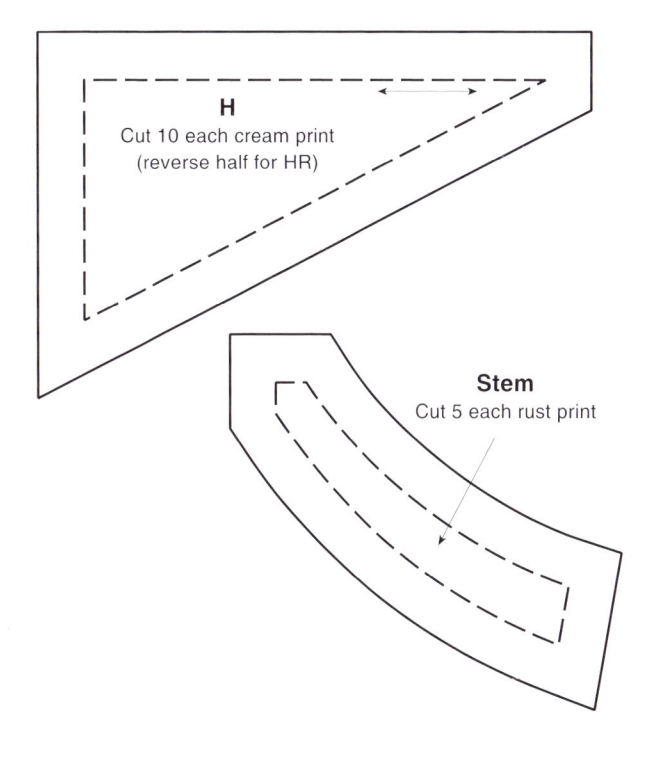

H
Cut 10 each cream print
(reverse half for HR)

Stem
Cut 5 each rust print

Scrappy Scarecrow

This scarecrow annouces to the world "A quilter lives here."

PROJECT NOTES
Create a stand for the scarecrow using an 11" candlestick base topped with a 17" length of ⅞" wooden dowel for the body (28" tall). Drill a ¼" hole through the dowel 5½" from the top and insert a 16" length of ¼" wooden dowel for arms. Add a wider piece on the bottom for more stability.

PROJECT SPECIFICATIONS
Skill Level: Advanced
Size: Approximately 19" x 28"

FABRIC & BATTING
- Scraps purple stripe, tan/white check, brown/black check, bright green tonal, rust and rose tonals and rust print
- Scraps 6 or 7 purple prints
- ¼ yard each 4 light orange prints or tonals
- ¼ yard each 3 dark orange prints or tonals
- ¼ yard light green tonal
- ⅓ yard flannel
- ⅓ yard purple print for vest lining
- ⅜ yard medium green print
- ½ yard orange check
- ⅝ yard muslin
- Batting scraps

SUPPLIES & TOOLS
- All-purpose thread to match fabrics
- Black No. 3 pearl cotton
- Black embroidery floss
- 2 (½") flat black buttons
- 5 (½") green buttons
- Clear fabric glue
- Raffia
- Scrap polyester fiberfill
- Pinking shears
- Basic sewing tools and supplies

Pants Patchwork
Note: All seams are ¼" unless otherwise noted. Some shapes are given without seam allowance so that stitching lines can be traced and stitched on. Secure ends of stitching for clothing and head construction.

1. Cut two 5" x 11" A pieces medium green print.

2. Cut three 2" x 35" strips each light green tonal (B) and medium green print (C).

3. Join the B and C strips in alternating order with right sides together along the length; press seams toward C.

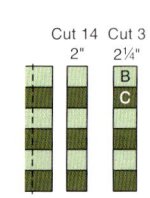

4. Subcut the strip set into (14) 2" and three 2¼" segments as shown in Figure 1.

Figure 1

5. Join the 2" B-C segments end to end to make a continuous length; press seams toward C. Repeat with the 2¼" B-C segments.

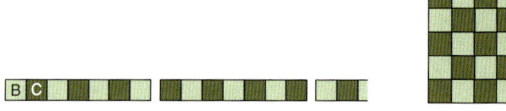

Figure 2 **Figure 3**

6. Separate the 2" joined B-C strip into seven-segment lengths as shown in Figure 2.

7. Join six 7-segment lengths, alternating colors beginning with a B piece on the first strip to make a leg unit as shown in Figure 3; repeat to make two leg units.

8. Separate the 2¼" joined B-C strip into two

seven-segment lengths as in step 6 with B pieces at each end of each segment as shown in Figure 4.

Figure 4

9. Sew a 2¼" strip to the bottom edge of each leg unit referring to Figure 5; press seams away from the 2¼" segments.

Figure 5

10. Sew an A piece to the top edge of each leg unit, again referring to Figure 5.

11. Cut two 10¾" x 15" muslin lining pieces and two 10¾" x 10½" batting pieces.

12. Center a batting piece 2½" below the top of a leg unit as shown in Figure 6; center a lining piece on top.

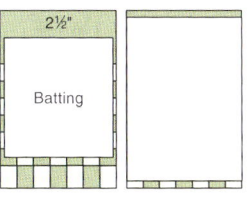

Figure 6

13. Machine-quilt in the ditch of all seams on the pieced leg units, extending square grid onto the A piece.

14. Prepare pants pattern. Center pattern at upper edge; trace cutting line onto each quilted

HOUSE OF WHITE BIRCHES, BERNE, INDIANA 46711 DRGNETWORK.COM   Autumn Harvest Quilts **37** leg unit. Trim away excess at crotch and leg edge, as shown in Figure 7.

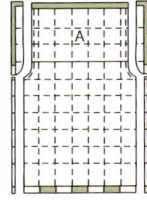

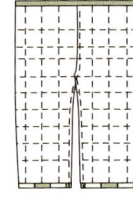

Figure 7

Figure 8

15. Press under 1½" at each leg bottom and A top for hem; unfold.

16. Join the leg sections at the center front and center back seams as shown in Figure 8; press seams open.

17. Join leg seam with crotch seams aligned, again referring to Figure 8; press seam open. Turn right side out; refold hem creases.

18. Using black pearl cotton, gather-stitch 1¼" above bottom folded edge beginning at the outside edge of both legs; repeat 1¼" below A top edge beginning in the center front for the waist. Cinch each leg in approximately 1½"; tie securely with decorative bow knots and ends. Cinch in waist approximately 1"; tie to complete pants.

19. Attach the center back top edge of the pants to the vertical dowel of the candlestick stand with leg bottoms approximately 1¼" above the surface of the table.

Triangle Foundation Patchwork
1. Make copies of the triangle paper-foundation pattern as indicated on pattern; trim eight patterns just beyond the outer solid line. Cut out three individual squares from the remaining pattern.

2. Cut two 6" x 9" rectangles and one 3" x 3" square from each of the four light (D) and three dark (E) orange prints or tonals and orange check (E). Pair a light piece right sides together with a dark or check piece with corresponding paper-foundation pattern print side up on top; pin. Repeat with all pieces.

3. Adjust machine to 8–10 stitches per inch; stitch through layers on dashed lines.

4. Rotary-cut sections apart on all solid lines to yield 102 D-E triangles; press open toward E to complete the D-E square units. Remove paper by folding and perforating along stitching lines; trim all triangle tails as shown in Figure 9.

Figure 9

Figure 10

Completing Sleeves & Shirt
1. Cut two 1½" x 6½" F strips orange check.

2. Arrange 30 D-E units in a pleasing alternating order to form two sleeves with five rows of three units each as shown in Figure 10; join units to make rows. Press seams in rows in alternating directions.

3. Join the rows to complete two sleeve units; press seams in one direction.

4. Sew an F strip to the bottom of each sleeve unit, again referring to Figure 10.

5. Cut two 7" x 9" batting pieces and two 7" x 12" muslin lining pieces.

6. Layer one each sleeve, batting and lining pieces with top edges even; pin.

7. Machine-quilt in the ditch along all seams, extending into unbatted areas; trim excess batting and lining even with patchwork top edges.

8. Press under a 1½" hem at the F end; unfold. Join the two sections on the pieced ends to make one long strip, leaving 1¾" open in the center as shown in Figure 11; press seam open.
Note: *The unfolded F strips will now be on each*

38 Autumn Harvest Quilts HOUSE OF WHITE BIRCHES, BERNE, INDIANA 46711 DRGNETWORK.COM

end of the joined strip. The opening is for the stand dowel to go through for the head.

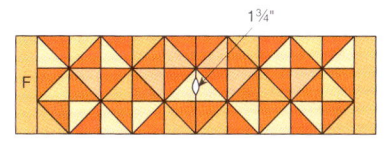

Figure 11

9. Fold the sleeve strip right sides together along the length; stitch along raw edges, leaving a 3" opening in the center as shown in Figure 12; press seam open. Turn right side out.

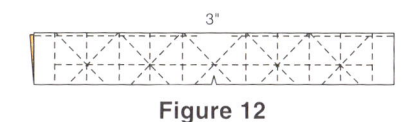

Figure 12

10. Refold the pressed hems at the F ends; gather-stitch as for leg sections 1¼" from folded edge, beginning at the sleeve center. Cinch in sleeve approximately 1"; tie to secure.

11. Cut (12) 1¼" x 2½" G strips from a variety of light and dark orange prints or tonals.

12. Arrange six G strips with 36 D-E units into three rows of five units and three rows of seven units referring to Figure 13; join in rows. Press seams in adjoining rows in alternating directions.

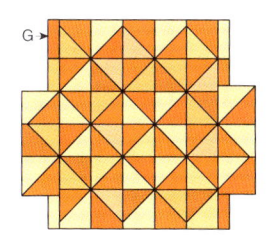

Figure 13

13. Join the rows to complete the front unit; press seams in one direction. Repeat to complete the back unit.

14. Cut muslin lining and batting pieces slightly larger than the pieced front and back units using the pieced units as a pattern; layer and quilt in the ditch of all seams.

15. Prepare shirt pattern. Center and trace pattern on each quilted section as shown in Figure 14; cut out.

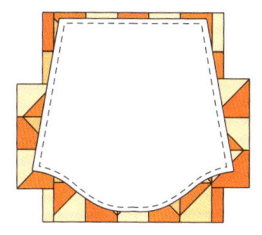

Figure 14

16. Cut a 2½" x 11½" H strip orange check for front placket strip. Press long edges in to meet at the center as shown in Figure 15.

Figure 15 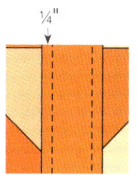   **Figure 16**

17. Center H on the right side of the front shirt section; trim excess length. Pin and then topstitch in place a generous ¼" from each edge to complete the shirt front as shown in Figure 16.

Vest Patchwork & Construction

1. Prepare one vest foundation pattern and one reverse vest foundation pattern as shown in Figure 17; trim foundations just beyond the outer solid line.

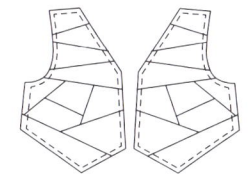

Figure 17

2. Complete foundation piecing in a crazy-patch style using random-size purple scraps. Trim patchwork on outer solid lines of foundation.

3. Use foundation patterns to cut flannel pieces. Remove paper foundations.

4. Place crazy-patchwork vest pieces on the flannel; machine-quilt in the ditch of all seams.

5. Cut one each purple stripe pocket and pocket lining. Join straight ends; press toward lining. Fold right sides together with bottom points aligned. Stitch, leaving an opening on one side; turn right side out and press.

6. Position and pin pocket to the left vest front as indicated on vest pattern.

7. Cut one 4" x 4" square bright green tonal for handkerchief. Fold in half diagonally with wrong sides together, and then pleat to create a pleasing point as shown in Figure 18. Insert behind pocket, re-pinning pocket as necessary. Topstitch pocket across placket seam and along sides as shown in Figure 19.

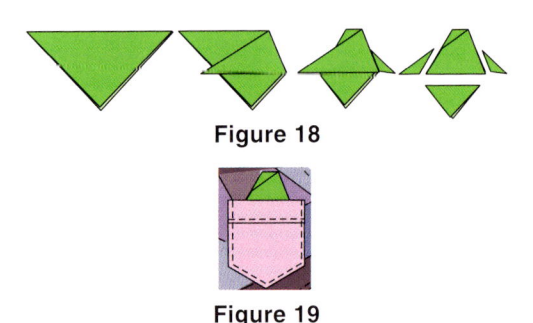

Figure 18

Figure 19

8. Use vest pieces to cut purple print lining pieces. Layer vest pieces with lining pieces right sides together; stitch around, leaving shoulder and side seams open.

9. Clip armhole curve seam allowance; turn right side out.

10. Press and topstitch ⅛" from edges all around stitched edges. **Note:** *Shoulder and side seams are still unstitched.*

11. Place the vest pieces right side up on the right side of the shirt front, matching shoulder and side edges; pin to hold.

12. Place the shirt back right sides together with the shirt front/vest piece. Join the pieces at the shoulders with right sides together, leaving 2" unstitched in the center as shown in Figure 20; press seam open.

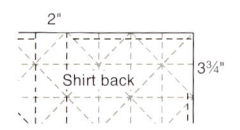

Figure 20

13. Join front to back at side edges with a ⅜" seam allowance, stopping 3¾" below shoulder seam, again referring to Figure 20. Press seam open. Fold armhole edges in ⅜"; press. Whipstitch raw edge to the lining to finish armholes.

14. Cut and join 2¼"-wide orange check bias strips to make a 29"-length for binding. Fold binding strip in half with wrong sides together along the length; press.

15. Pin the folded binding strip to the bottom raw edge of the shirt with raw edges even beginning in the center back; stitch, overlapping at the beginning and end. Turn the binding to the inside; hand- or machine-stitch in place to finish edges.

16. Sew the ½" green buttons to the shirt placket strip 1" from top at 2" intervals.

17. To assemble shirt, insert and center sleeve tube through the arm opening in the shirt.

Head Assembly

1. Prepare a 6½" x 13" sandwich of tan/white check, batting and muslin; machine-quilt a 1" diagonal grid.

2. Trace and cut two head pieces from the quilted section.

3. Transfer facial features to the head front; backstitch the mouth using 2 strands black embroidery floss.

4. Place the head pieces right sides together; stitch around sides and top, leaving bottom edges open; trim seam allowance to ⅛"; turn right side out. Press.

5. Trim neck opening with pinking shears.

6. Cut one nose from rust tonal using pattern given; fold ¼" under all around. Position and hand-appliqué in place on face front.

7. Prepare a 2¼" x 4" sandwich of rose tonal, batting and rose tonal; quilt a ½" diagonal grid. Center and trace two cheeks onto the quilted section using pattern given.

8. Using pinking shears, cut out cheeks ³⁄₁₆" beyond traced lines.

9. Glue cheeks and black-button eyes in place on face using clear fabric glue.

10. Prepare a 7" x 9" sandwich of rust print, batting and rust print for hair. Quilt with matching thread as shown on pattern. Trace pattern onto the quilted piece; topstitch on the marked lines. Using pinking shears, cut out ³⁄₁₆" beyond stitching.

11. Center the back side of the head over the hair piece; secure in place using clear fabric glue.

12. Fold front "fringe" over the top of the head; secure in place using clear fabric glue.

13. Prepare a sandwich using brown/black check, batting and brown/black check 4" x 10" for hat crowns and 5" x 8" for hat brims. Quilt in a ½" grid or following lines in the fabric; trace pattern on the quilted pieces.

14. Cut out two hat crown pieces; layer with right sides together and stitch around sides and top, leaving bottom edge open. Trim ⅛" beyond stitching; turn right side out and press flat.

15. Trace two hat brim shapes on brim section. Topstitch on traced lines and use pinking shears to cut out ³⁄₁₆" beyond stitching.

16. Layer brims and stitch together along lower curve; insert hat crown lower edges into the open top of the brim piece and secure in place using clear fabric glue.

17. Place the hat behind the head/hair unit and secure in place with clear fabric glue.

18. Place a wad of polyester fiberfill inside the top of the head.

19. Cut two 3¼" x 11" pieces orange check and one flannel; layer with orange check pieces right sides together and flannel on the bottom.

20. Trace collar pattern on the top piece; stitch all around on the marked line, leaving an opening on one side as marked on pattern. Trim

Scrappy Scarecrow
Placement Diagram
Approximately 19" x 28"

HOUSE OF WHITE BIRCHES, BERNE, INDIANA 46711   DRGNETWORK.COM

Autumn Harvest Quilts   **41**

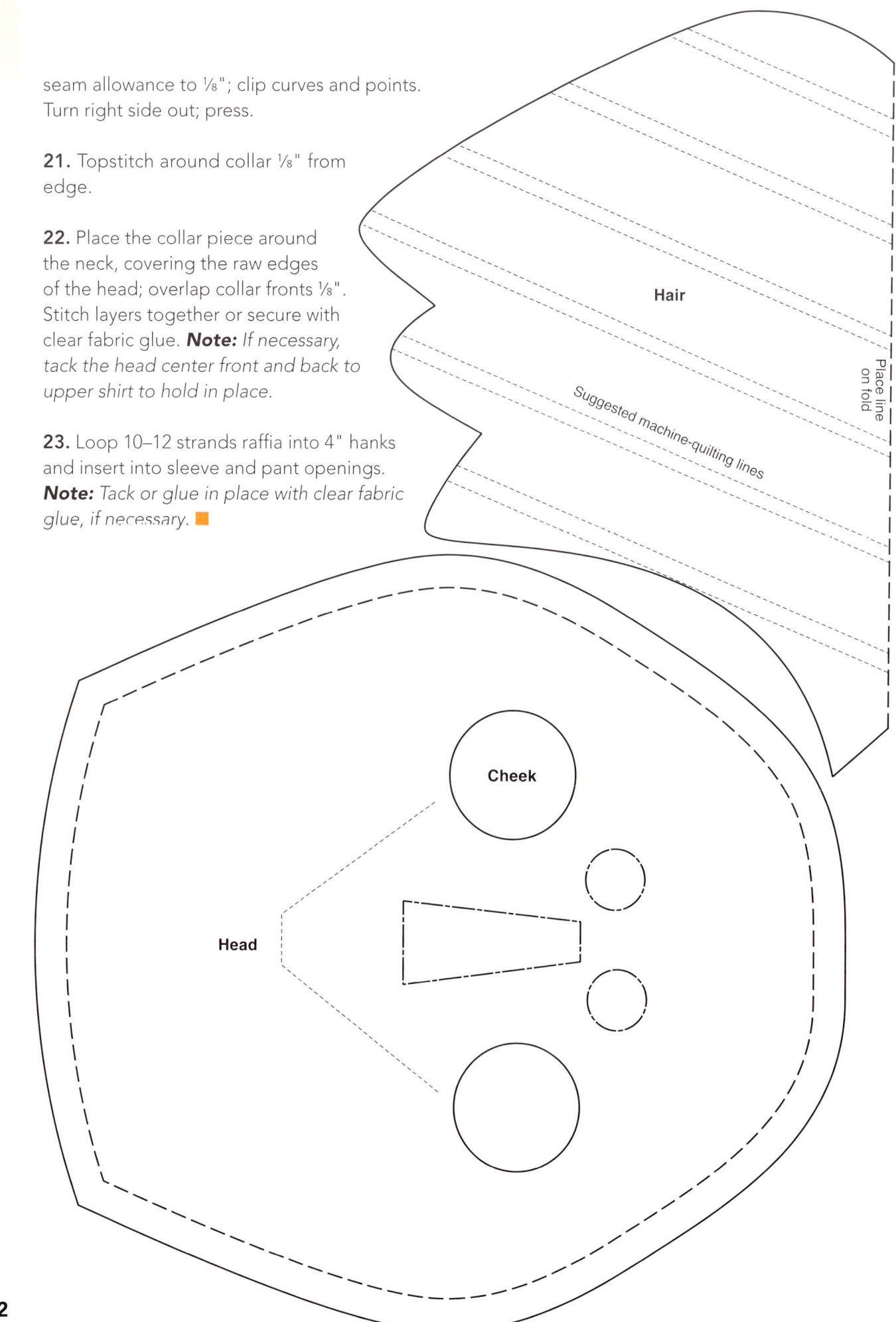

seam allowance to ⅛"; clip curves and points. Turn right side out; press.

21. Topstitch around collar ⅛" from edge.

22. Place the collar piece around the neck, covering the raw edges of the head; overlap collar fronts ⅛". Stitch layers together or secure with clear fabric glue. **Note:** *If necessary, tack the head center front and back to upper shirt to hold in place.*

23. Loop 10–12 strands raffia into 4" hanks and insert into sleeve and pant openings. **Note:** *Tack or glue in place with clear fabric glue, if necessary.* ◼

Hair

Place line on fold

Suggested machine-quilting lines

Cheek

Head

42

Nose
Cut 1
rust tonal

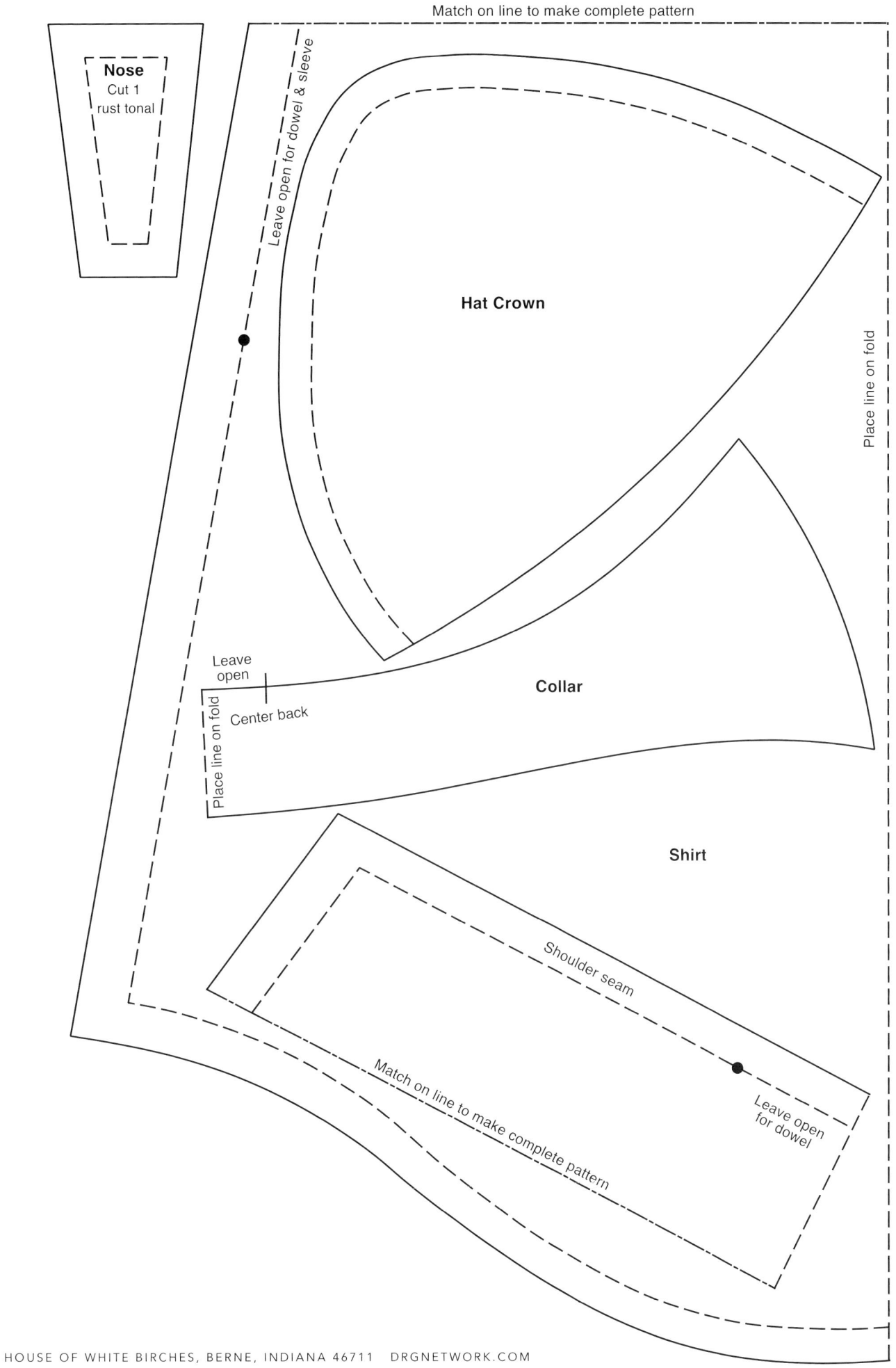

Match on line to make complete pattern

Leave open for dowel & sleeve

Hat Crown

Place line on fold

Leave open

Center back

Place line on fold

Collar

Shirt

Shoulder seam

Match on line to make complete pattern

Leave open for dowel

HOUSE OF WHITE BIRCHES, BERNE, INDIANA 46711   DRGNETWORK.COM

Hat Brim

Stitch front & back sections together along this edge between dots

Hem fold line

Pants

Match on line to make complete pattern
Add 6" between lines.

Hem fold line

44   Autumn Harvest Quilts

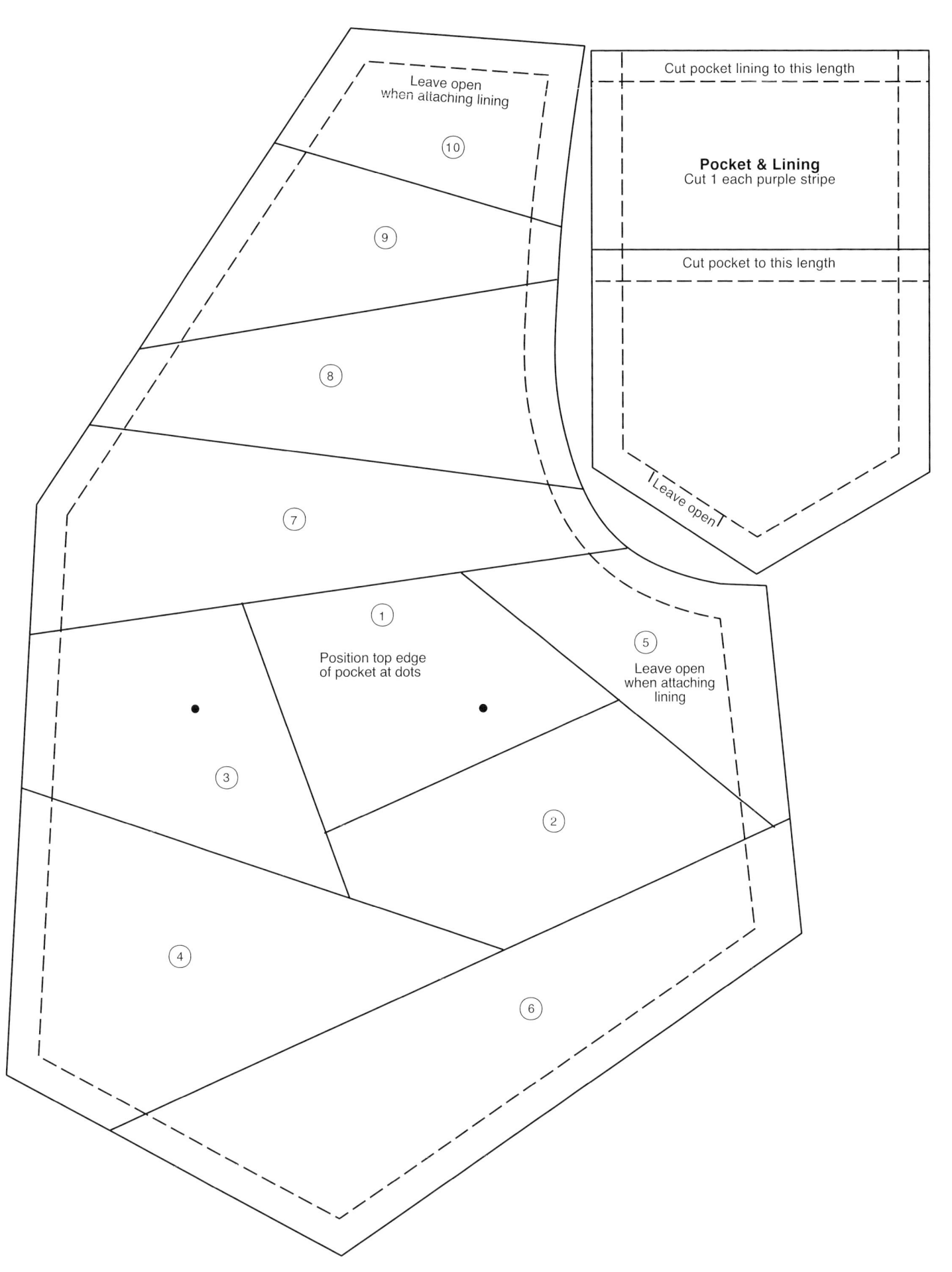

Vest Paper-Foundation Pattern
Make 2 copies
Right side shown; trace one copy through to the back side for left.

Autumn Harvest Quilts 45

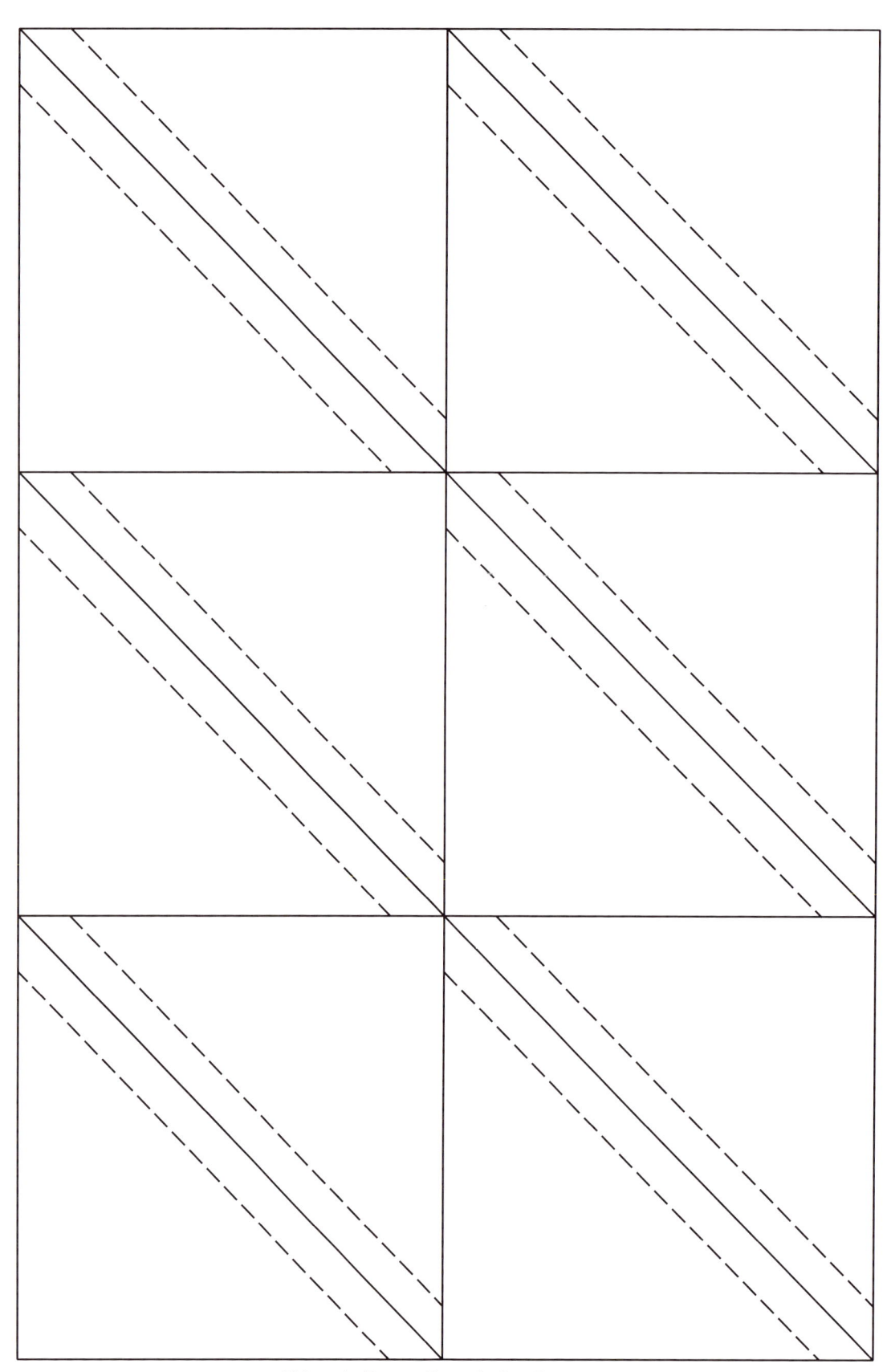

Triangle Paper-Foundation Pattern
Make 9 copies
Stitch on dashed lines; cut on solid lines.

Paper-Piecing Instructions

1. Cut apart one copy of each paper-piecing pattern given to make templates for each piece.

2. Place a paper template with the unmarked side of the paper on the wrong side of the chosen fabric; cut out, leaving at least a ¼" seam allowance all around as shown in Figure 1. Any excess will be trimmed after sewing.

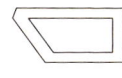

Figure 1

3. Pin fabric piece 1 right side up on the unprinted side of the paper-piecing pattern, covering area 1 as shown in Figure 2.

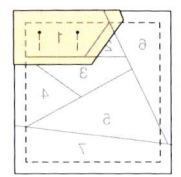

Figure 2   **Figure 3**

4. Turn the pinned unit to the marked side of the paper and hold it up to a light source to check to see if the fabric will cover area 1 and extend at least ¼" into adjacent areas as shown in Figure 3.

5. Pin fabric piece 2 right side down on the top of fabric piece 1; fold back and repeat step 4 to check that piece 2 will cover area 2 after stitching.

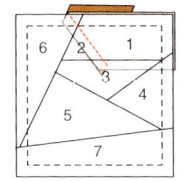

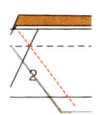

Figure 4   **Figure 5**

6. Using a very small machine stitch (1.5mm or 18–20 stitches per inch), stitch along the marked line between areas 1 and 2 as shown in Figure 4, extending stitching 1–2 stitches into adjacent areas and to the outer solid line of the pattern for outside pieces as shown in Figure 5.

7. Turn paper over and trim the seam allowance to ¼" as shown in Figure 6; flip piece 2 to the right side and press flat to cover area 2 as shown in Figure 7.

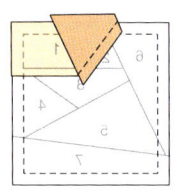

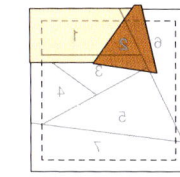

Figure 6   **Figure 7**

8. Align fabric piece 3 right sides together on the 1-2-3 edge; flip the paper to the printed side and sew on the lines between pieces 2 and 3; trim seam and press piece 3 to the right side.

9. Continue adding patches until the paper foundation unit is complete. Trim edges even with outside line of paper pattern as shown in Figure 8 to complete the unit.

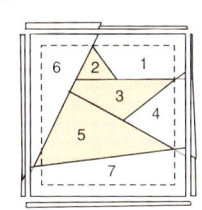

Figure 8

10. For designs that have more than one paper-pieced section, such as the house peak in Autumn Rows, repeat steps 1–9 for each section.

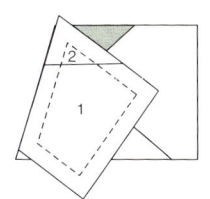

Figure 9

11. To join paper-pieced units, identify several key matching points between the units/sections; pin through the layers at these points to align as shown in Figure 9. Stitch to join; remove paper from seam allowance of the stitched seam and press to one side. ■

HOUSE OF WHITE BIRCHES, BERNE, INDIANA 46711   DRGNETWORK.COM   Autumn Harvest Quilts

Meet the Designer
Jodi G. Warner

Jodi G. Warner finds inspiration and creative time in her home studio in a rural/residential area near Salt Lake City, Utah. Working within easy reach of family members and near treasured quilts and other keepsakes, she finds it especially enjoyable to execute her designs in fabric and stitches.

Jodi was raised in the Holladay community southeast of Salt Lake City. She learned to sew at a very young age. She received a B.A. degree in Textiles/Fashion Design from Brigham Young University in 1978, and began designing and making costumes for a theatrical studio and gowns for a bridal shop.

As a new homemaker, Jodi found she enjoyed applying traditional patchwork and appliqué methods to solve home decorating needs. She soon realized she had found a design arena that offered endless challenges and rewards.

Jodi has lectured, conducted workshops, taught at quilt shops and mounted one-woman quilt shows throughout the Intermountain West. Jodi's quilts have won local, regional and national honor, including several prestigious purchase awards. Her patterns and articles about her work have appeared in many magazines. She also owns and operates her own pattern business, Hearthsewn, a natural outgrowth of the requests from students and area shops for formalized patterns of the designs she was teaching. Many cherished quilting memories involve sharing with students what she has learned and developed, with the dividend being a faithful student following.

One of Jodi's ongoing interests centers around a growing collection of quilts paired with children's storybooks, which she uses to promote family literacy and quiltmaking awareness.

Oak & Acorn Pillow
continued from page 12

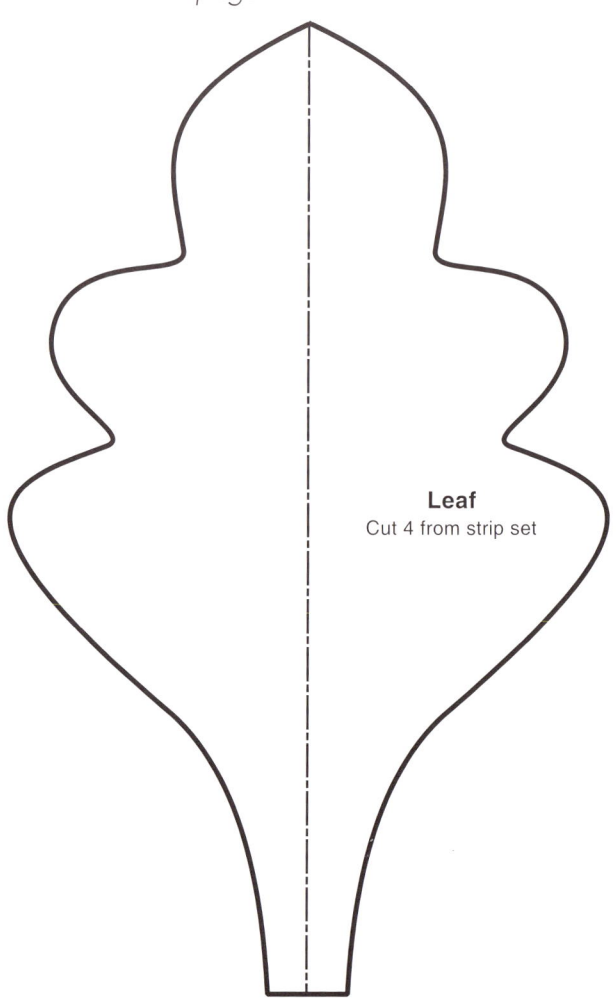

Leaf
Cut 4 from strip set

E-mail: Customer_Service@DRGnetwork.com

Autumn Harvest Quilts is published by DRG, 306 East Parr Road, Berne, IN 46711, telephone (260) 589-4000. Printed in USA. Copyright © 2007 DRG. All rights reserved. This publication may not be reproduced in part or in whole without written permission from the publisher.

RETAIL STORES: If you would like to carry this pattern book or any other DRG publications, call the Wholesale Department at Annie's Attic to set up a direct account: (903) 636-4303. Also, request a complete listing of publications available from DRG.

Every effort has been made to ensure that the instructions in this pattern book are complete and accurate. We cannot, however, take responsibility for human error, typographical mistakes or variations in individual work.

HOUSE of WHITE BIRCHES
PUBLISHERS SINCE 1947

ISBN: 978-1-59217-163-7
1 2 3 4 5 6 7 8 9

STAFF
Editors: Jeanne Stauffer, Sandra L. Hatch
Managing Editor: Dianne Schmidt
Technical Artist: Connie Rand
Copy Supervisor: Michelle Beck
Copy Editors: Sue Harvey, Nicki Lehman, Mary O'Donnell, Judy Weatherford
Graphic Arts Supervisor: Ronda Bechinski
Graphic Artists: Nicole Gage
Art Director: Brad Snow
Assistant Art Director: Nick Pierce
Photography: Tammy Christian, Don Clark, Matthew Owen, Jackie Schaffel
Photo Stylists: Tammy Nussbaum, Tammy M. Smith